This Is The Thanks I Get?

A Guide to Raising Teenagers

This Is The Thanks I Get?

A Guide to Raising Teenagers

· by Wayne Rickerson ·

STANDARD PUBLISHING
Cincinnati, Ohio   29-03152

ISBN 0-87403-406-X

Contents

Introduction

So you're the parent of a teenager. You can see pity in the eyes of the persons you've been talking to. They have paid their dues. Their teenagers are young adults now, but they still remember the turmoil caused by adolescence and their hearts reach out to you.

I don't want sympathy, you think to yourself. *I want help. I want to know how I can cope with my own feelings and help my teenagers through their own emotional turmoil.*

In this book, I try to provide help for parents of teenagers in three ways. First, I have sorted through my own feelings of guilt, inadequacy, frustration, and anger, and offer some suggestions on how to deal with these emotions. Second, I take a close look at the struggles a teenager must go through. Many of our frustrations as parents stem from a lack of understanding of the tremendous physical, emotional, social, and spiritual adjustments our teenagers must make. Third, I offer some practical advice on how to guide our teenagers through the maze of adolescent obstacles.

No book has *all* the answers for *every* parent. Each teenager is unique. No two parents are the same. In this book I share with you the things that have helped Janet and me become more effective with teenagers. We fall short of some of the very principles we advocate in this book. We do not set ourselves up as model parents of teenagers. We are fellow strugglers with you, in attempting to let God control our lives as we help our children develop mature Christian consciences.

You can use this book in four basic ways. First, you can read it yourself and answer the questions that follow each chapter. I strongly recommend you answer the questions, because they will cause you to probe deep into your own spirit. The questions will also help you make some decisions and apply what you are reading to your life.

A second way of using this book is to read the book together with your spouse and answer the questions at the end of each chapter separately. Take some time for just the two of you to discuss the answers to your questions. Make some decision together on how you will handle your teenagers.

A third way to use this book is in a 13-week course format. I have written a Leaders Guide that gives a simple, practical approach for teaching the concepts in this book. You can use this Leaders Guide in a Bible-school class, as a Sunday evening or weeknight elective, or as an aid to parenting groups.

A fourth way to use this book is in a small parenting group. I recommend forming small groups of not more than ten parents of teenagers to meet weekly and discuss the material in this book. The discussion questions at the end of each chapter are designed for group use. By sharing with other parents, we receive encouragement and support and we learn from one another.

How to Form Parenting Groups

The plan is simple. First you elect a group leader or leaders, depending on how many groups you want to form. I suggest using couples when possible. The couple ideally should be one who has raised or is raising teenagers and has done an effective job with them. That is not to say they should be "perfect parents." *There is no such species.*

Such a person, if he existed, would be ill-fitted to deal with the rest of us mortal parents who make a few too many mistakes. The leaders should be persons who are willing to share their defeats as well as their victories.

Next you find a group of parents who would like to develop some insights into guiding teenagers. *There are a lot of such people around.* There should be a minimum of five and a maximum of twelve parents in your group.

Next you decide what schedule fits your church program. If you have existing family groups that meet regularly and are age-graded, then I suggest you use these existing groups and times. If you do not have this situation then you will need to form separate parenting groups. It works well to have these groups meet in homes.

This book is divided into three sections of four, five, and four chapters each. Unless the group is meeting during the Bible-school hour, it is best to have the parenting groups meet for shorter times rather than the full thirteen sessions.

If you choose the small-group format, I suggest you run your first group for four weeks, covering the basic material in the section, *Laying a Firm Foundation—Increasing Understanding.* At the end of this time, ask the group if they would like to set a time to study the next section on *Building the Structure—Developing Skills.* If they choose to meet again you can again find the interest level for the final section, *The Finishing Touches.*

How to Lead a Parenting Group

The group sessions are very simple. Each couple or person gets a book. Before the group session, everyone reads the chapter and answers the questions at the end of the chapter. The group leaders (a husband/wife team, if possible) answer the same questions. The group then shares the answers to their questions as the group leader guides the conversation. I suggest one-to two-hour sessions.

It is generally a good rule to start with Question One, because it is designed to be an "opener" to the general topic. There is no way you will cover all the questions in one hour. It is possible in two hours. The purpose of the questions is to help parents look into their own lives and make some personal applications. Not all of this has to be shared with the group. *Choose the questions that you feel are important for your group to cover.*

Several ingredients make parenting groups effective. Encouragement and support are vital. Another important element is input. Parents receive their initial input by reading the chapters. More input comes from the other parents during the sessions. Introspection is also necessary. Introspection occurs as individuals answer the questions at the end of each chapter. This causes them to examine themselves.

Sharing is a very important part of the process. Through sharing, I hear myself. As I verbalize I can start putting my own problems into perspective. I get insights into myself and my parenting problems. You have probably had that experience already. You have a problem and you ask a friend to help you solve it. You start talking and by the time you're finished you thank your friend for helping you solve your problem. He says, "I didn't say a word!" By verbalizing your problem to someone who cared, you were able to solve it your own problem.

A final ingredient that will make your parenting group effective is application. The last question on every discussion page asks the parent to commit himself to some kind of specific plan to change. This is essential. Simply knowing facts or Biblical insights will not insure growth. Only when we *apply* those principles to our lives will real growth occur.

At the end of your parenting sessions, suggest that couples go home and decide together on what changes need to be made within their homes.

One last word of encouragement—Janet and I are excited about the opportunity God has given us to *grow with our teenagers* Through the pain and frustrations, we have seen God's hand building maturity in our own lives. While there is no denying the anxieties that accompany raising children, there can be a great deal of joy as we see our children mature. *I am glad that God gave me the opportunity to be a parent.* May God bless your pilgrimage through this book!

Section One

Laying a Firm Foundation— Increasing Understanding

CHAPTER 1

How Can We Be Prepared?

We can't be totally prepared for the teenage years. We can read books, listen to tapes, listen to the horror stories of friends, but we lack the real emotions until we actually live with a teenager. This chapter will help you deal with these emotions. You are not the only parent that experiences feelings of fear, anger, despair, resentment, lack of control, guilt, and the other emotions that come with the territory.

Negative emotions are not the only ones we feel as parents of teenagers. There are positive emotions of pride, joy, elation, trust, thankfulness. For the most part Janet and I have really enjoyed our teenage girls. But negative emotions can give us trouble. Occasionally we wonder where a parent of a teenager can go to resign.

Since resigning is not the answer, let's consider some constructive ways of handling our emotions. We will look at feeling afraid, threatened, not in control, angry, resentful, guilty, and low in self-esteem.

Negative Emotions

My Family Is Out of Control (feelings of fear)
When our children are young we have a strong sense of

control. They need us desperately to survive. We provide them with their basic needs—food, shelter, protection, and love. We are certain, in spite of occasional threats, that they are not going to run away. They need us. Then comes adolescence and the feeling that we can no longer control teens as we did when they were younger. We are keenly aware that we must take seriously a threat to run away. It is possible for them to leave home and survive. Thousands of teenagers do every year.

Our teens no longer unquestioningly accept our values. We are questioned, sometimes challenged. Family time is no longer as important to our teenagers as it was when they were in grade school. They seem content to spend time by themselves or with friends. It seems that it is more important to our teenagers to please their friends than it is to please us.

"What is happening to our family?" we ask ourselves. *We are losing control!* This loss of control can make us feel fearful and threatened. Janet and I certainly have experienced these feelings. It has helped us, however, to realize that a host of other parents of teenagers experience the same feelings. It is also consoling to know that what our teenagers are going through is a part of God's plan for their lives. To help us understand God's plan I would like to share with you the three phases of the parent-child relationship.

Phase 1—Bonding: During the early years of our children's lives we go through a bonding process. As loving parents we build a close relationship with our children. We meet their physical needs. We meet their emotional needs by giving them emotional support and physical affection. By our actions our children feel secure and loved within the family circle. We are in control. They are dependent upon us for their existence.

Phase 2—Debonding: For a teenager to successfully complete the pilgrimage from dependence to independence, he must "debond" from his parents. Debonding takes place as our teens pull back emotionally from us. They demand more time by themselves or with friends.

14

They argue against our "old-fashioned standards." Their speech and dress indicate that they are in the process of debonding.

This is necessary. There is nothing more pitiful than a young adult that is still bonded to his parents. They never achieve their own sense of self—never become the mature, confident adults that God intended for them to become.

If we fight against the debonding process, we enter an unnecessary war and are actually defying God's plan for human development. Scripture indicates that Jesus himself went through the human process of debonding as He "... continued to grow and become strong, increasing in wisdom; and the grace of God was upon Him" (Luke 2:40). This same passage tells the story of how Jesus, when He was twelve (entering the debonding years), went with His parents to the temple in Jerusalem. On the return trip home, Jesus' parents realized He was not with the caravan. They returned to Jerusalem and found Him in the temple asking questions of the teachers. Their response was typical of what ours might be. Jesus' mother said, "Son, why have You treated us this way? Behold, Your father and I have been anxiously looking for You" v. 48).

In this Scripture passage we see both Jesus' humanity and His divinity. Jesus was in the "debonding" stage of human development and His parents were anxious.

Phase 3—Rebonding: After your teenager leaves home, a natural rebonding occurs. He is now independent and has a well established identity; he no longer feels it necessary to pull away from you. The task has been completed. A new, warm, mature relationship emerges.

Bonding, debonding, and rebonding are all part of a natural, healthy process. Remembering these stages can help us when we struggle with the feeling that we are losing control of our family.

How Can They Do This to Me?
(feelings of anger)

I detect a bit of anger in Mary's question, "Son, why have You treated us this way?" I can certainly identify with her, for I think this is a natural response to some of the frustrations of raising a teenager. Let's face it, we have poured our lives into our children. They have been a high priority. We have sacrificed for them, prayed and agonized for their future. We have committed ourselves to help them achieve happy Christian lives, and it looks, at times, like they couldn't care less. It is natural for us to be disappointed when it looks as if all our work has gone down the drain.

It is natural to experience the emotion of anger, but it is unhealthy to be controlled by it. Anger controls us when we repress it or make actions of aggression. There is a difference between feelings of anger and actions of anger. The appropriate handling of our anger is an important aspect of teenage parenting. In a later chapter on communication, we will look at ways to handle our anger.

It is frustrating when our teens don't appreciate what we are doing for them, but it is good to remember this: "Teenagers are not grateful when parents act wisely—when parents know whether to give emotional support or hold back. The satisfaction has to come from the parent's own joy in knowing they are doing the right thing."[1]

As we raise our teens it seems that we must do an unfair amount of giving to the relationship. Janet and I were recently talking to some wise Christian friends who have teenagers. We mentioned that it concerned us that our teens seldom came to us and asked for forgiveness, even though we ask them for forgiveness for our mistakes.

"Our teenagers seldom come to us to ask forgiveness," they replied. "We finally decided not to expect it. We have modeled this quality for them, but we are going to have to wait to see it in their lives."

God has assigned parents the task of leadership in the family. At times, it seems we are a little shortchanged, but the day will come when we will see the fruits of our work. I love what Dr. John Claypool, pastor of Northminster Baptist Church, Jackson, Mississippi, says.

There is a word every parent needs to hear during the adolescent era of his child's life. Just as a seed disappears for a period of time, and you begin to fear it is lost altogether, so there is a time in a child's life when it seems that all the efforts of parents are for nothing. Not so! If there has been a faithful sowing of the seed during the long days and nights of childhood, a harvest of healthy personhood will likely emerge. This does not mean that one's children will come out carbon copies of their parents, for this would ill equip them for living in their own day. Rather, it means they will be able to cope creatively and responsibly with life, which is all any parent should want.[2]

I Am an Inadequate Parent!
(feelings of guilt and low self-esteem)

Many times during our children's teenage years I have felt inadequate as a parent. At times I have felt like a failure. There are new feelings for me, for most of my life I prided myself on being an exceptional parent. God has a way of taking care of pride.

When we have problems with our teenagers, a normal reaction is to try to place blame. We either blame ourselves or our teens. This is a destructive way of dealing with a problem. Actually, we both share the responsibility. "God would be unjust in punishing sin if we were not personally responsible for our actions. The fact that we bear a great responsibility for our children does not erase the fact that our children also have a say in their own destiny. Scripture speaks specifically to the responsibility of children.

> Even a child is known by his actions,
> by whether his conduct is pure and right.
> Proverbs 20:11, *NIV*

> Children, obey your parents in the Lord,
> for this is right.   Ephesians 6:1[3]

"That both parent and child bear a share of the responsibility follows logically from the facts that both parent and child are sinners and are moral beings. Each party, however, shares a different aspect of responsibility. We are instructed to provide for our children's needs and train them properly. Children, in turn, are responsible for following our leadership and accepting increasing personal responsibility as they mature."[4]

God does not want us to take total responsibility for either our children's achievements or failures. To do so would deny both God's activity in their lives and their free will to choose.

We are accountable to teach them the Word of God, discipline them, unconditionally love and accept them, and give them our best. Our children, however, are responsible for their own lives. We provide them with the gift of our Christian parenting. They must do something with that gift. They must properly use it. No one can help someone who refuses help. We have a huge impact on our children's lives. No one will deny that. Good parenting usually produces good children. Poor parenting usually produces problem children. This is no ironclad rule. We all can think of exceptions to the rule.

All God expects of us is to commit ourselves sacrificially to the task of parenting. Feelings of inadequacy and low self-esteem will still visit us occasionally. Conflict often brings those emotions to the surface. When problems and conflict occur, we must always be willing to look at ourselves, but at the same time, we must acknowledge our teen's responsibility and God's influence in their lives.

Three Vital Relationships

You must develop three vital relationships if you are going to be effective parents of teenagers. I believe these are the foundation of good parenting. These relationships are with God, with your spouse, and with your teen.

Your Relationship With God

All family relationships are based on the quality of your relationship with God. This starts when you are born into the family of God through placing your trust in Jesus. This is only the beginning. We are born into the family of God as babes, but we are expected to grow toward maturity in Christ. God has given us a food that never fails to produce maturity, His Word. A daily diet of His Word gives us growth necessary for the other vital relationships in our life. "All Scripture is inspired by God and profitable for teaching, for reproof, for correction, for training in righteousness; that the man of God may be adequate, equipped for every good work" (2 Timothy 3:16, 17).

God's Word will equip us for the "good work" of parenting. God's Word will build in us the character needed to become effective parents. We all have areas of our personality that hinder us in parenting. Mine is a quick temper and a lack of a gentle spirit. Through the "sword of the Spirit, which is the word of God" (Ephesians 6:17), God is working to slow my temper and build a gentle spirit in me.

I find that a daily diet of God's Word is an absolute necessity for me to be an effective parent. When I do not take enough time with the Lord each day, in the reading of God's Word, memorization, meditation, and prayer, I can tell the difference in my family relationships. The quick temper starts raising its ugly horns. The motivation for a gentle spirit starts to fade away.

Start a daily quiet time with the Lord, if you do not have one. If your quiet time lacks direction, here is a suggestion for a format.

Reading God's Word. Get a notebook with blank pieces of paper. Start with a book of the Bible and read a passage each day. Ask yourself the following questions about the passage.

—What does this passage tell me about God?
—What does this passage say to me?
—What does God want me to do?

Write out your answers. This helps you apply God's Word to your life. It is not what we know that is important, but how we apply what we know to our lives. God's Word is to be "lived out."

Memorization and meditation. Start by memorizing just one or two verses a week. Meditate on these verses. Meditation is visualizing the verses, mulling them over in your mind and applying them to your life. Your greatest spiritual growth will come from memorization and meditation.

Prayer. Write down specific prayer requests and then record them when God answers. Pray for your children every day. Janet and I, in addition to praying for the children each day, set aside one day each week for prayer and fasting for the children. We reserve some time during the day to pray together for our children.

Your Relationship With Your Spouse

Your relationship with God should be your highest priority in life. Your second highest priority should be your relationship with your spouse. Your third priority should be your relationship with your children. Sometimes we get our second and third priorities out of order. Janet and I did early in our marriage. The development of our relationship took a back seat to our relationship with our children. We recognized our mistake and started concentrating on our marriage relationship. This was not only the best thing we could have done for the two of us, but it was also the best thing we could have done for our children. The more we love one another, as husband and wife, the more our children feel loved and secure.

> Our whole relationship with our children is going to be different, if we focus on our spouse rather than our children. Sometimes we think that the more attention we pay directly to our children, the more they are going to feel loved and appreciated. Actually, the more absorbed that we are with one another, and the more the children continue to get their meaning from our relationship with one another, the more they are going to have.[5]

Janet and I have found that the teen years have brought some new stresses into our marriage. We have had to rediscuss some of our child rearing policies. As the rules have been tested, we have been tested. When things are going poorly with teenagers, it is a great temptation to blame one another for what's going on. Sometimes, Janet and I have disagreements over how to handle our children. During these stressful times we have stopped several times and agreed, *we are not going to let problems with our children damage our marriage relationship.* We are committed to working toward unity. "Problems with children have as great a potential to strengthen a marriage as to wreck it. They can bring you together in a new unity or blow you apart."[6]

When Janet and I decided to make our marriage the number two priority in our lives, we started having weekly "Together Times." For many years we met faithfully for a weekly time of discussion, planning, Bible reading, and prayer. This was a tremendous asset for our marriage. It reminded us each week of our commitment to growing closer to God and to one another. I believe that one of the reasons many marriages today lack closeness is that there is little quality husband and wife time. By quality time, I mean time that can be counted on each week for husband and wife to be alone and have meaningful talks.

> I cannot exaggerate the importance of parental harmony. Children need it, and need it more than ever when they go wrong. Their well-being depends on it. The welfare of children rests more on parental unity than on any child-rearing expertise the parents may have. Parents can get away with many mistakes if their children see them as a solid, loving alliance. Such an alliance creates a context in which children can respond with respect and obedience.[7]

Your Relationship With Your Teen

I believe that the critical point in parenting teenagers is to maintain a positive relationship with them. You notice I said, "maintain." This suggests that a warm, loving relationship has been built during the early years of "bonding." During some of the stormy years of adolescence I was glad that Janet and I committed ourselves to building family unity during those early years. The family was a high priority even during the strenuous years of college and seminary. We were committed not only to family time, but to building a personal relationship with each of the children. I can look back with no regrets at the amount of time and effort I spent with the children. Those positive relationships have a way of surviving the storms of adolescence. I look at the love and time we invested with the children as a "love bank account." We are now drawing on that bank account. If we had not made the proper investments, there would be very little to draw on during the teenage years. It is the loving relationship with Heidi, Liesl, and Bridget that brought us through the tight spots. The motivation for obedience is a result of the relationship.

Our heavenly Father builds His relationships with us in a similar manner. He first comes to us and offers us His love. Then based on this loving relationship He asks us to obey what is in His Word. If God asked us to obey before He offered us His love, we would have little motivation to respond. It is the same way in human relationships. If we build loving relationships with our children, they will be more likely to obey us from the motivation of love.

This does not mean all is lost if you have not built a loving relationship with your children during the bonding years. It does make it more difficult because they are by nature pulling away. Relationships can always be rebuilt. Love and forgiveness is an overpowering force that can break through the toughest barriers.

Just because we have built a bank account of loving relationships during the early years, we should not stop investing in the teenage years. While family time was not as important to our teenage girls as it once had been, I noticed that the one-on-one time was just as important. They still valued going someplace or doing something with Mom or Dad alone. They still needed unconditional love and acceptance. In some ways they needed it even more than in the early years. I was shocked one day during a painful confrontation with one of our daughters to hear that she felt unloved. "How can you feel that we don't love you after all these years of showing you love?" I asked, feeling hurt. I had to learn even though those feelings were temporary, they were real. The low self-esteem that accompanies adolescence can make teens feel worthless and unloved. We cannot take for granted that they feel loved. We must reassure them constantly. They still need tolerance and forgiveness. Here are some questions you can ask yourself, to see if you are still building a loving relationship with your teens.

—Do your teens feel that they have your unconditional love? Do they feel loved even when they are not responding as you would desire? Do you say "I love you" every day?

—Do you spend time listening (with interest) to what is important in their lives?

—How is your tolerance level? Do you try to understand their points of view? Are you sensitive to the turmoils of adolescence?

—Are you able to forgive—again and again and again? Are you willing to give your trust once more even though your teenager has acted in an untrustworthy manner?

Few could answer yes to all of the above questions. None of us are perfect parents. It's probably a good thing, because if we were, our children would be ill-prepared for life in an imperfect world. We can, however, aim for the above goals, always stretching ourselves to new and better relationships. We must understand our limitations and not feel destructive guilt when we fall short.

Howard Hendricks in his book, *Heaven Help the Home*, gives an illustration that can help us see how the three relationships, a vital relationship with God, with your spouse, and with your teen, all fit together.

> Do you love God? "Of course, every Christian loves God," you reply. OK. If we love God, then we must obey God. That's where the home begins. A man and a wife, each love-related to God through His Son, who is the expression of God's love to man. Each related to the other in human love and mutual trust.
>
> The strength of this triangle is invincible. The closer each partner moves toward God, the closer he is to the other.[8]

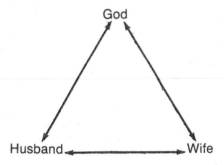

God

Husband Wife

Figure 1-1. Three Relationships

Now in the middle of the triangle I would like you to mentally write in the word *teenager.* Notice the effect. The closer you move to God (vital relationship with God), the closer both of you move toward your teenager (vital relationship with your teen).

God expects us to develop each of the three relationships. What God expects, He enables. We can count on God to give us the strength to build the kind of relationship within that He expects.

---

[1]Jean Rosenbaum and Veryl Rosenbaum, *Living With Teenagers*. New York: Stein and Day, 1980, p. 50.

[2]Dr. John Claypool, "Sowing and Praying: Warning and Promise." (Sermon given on January 15, 1978 at Northminister Baptist Church, Jackson, Mississippi.)

[3]Bruce Narramore, *Parenting With Love and Limits*. Grand Rapids, MI: Zondervan, 1979, p. 142.

[4]Narramore, p. 143.

[5]Chuck Gallagher, *Parents Are Lovers*. New York: Doubleday, 1977, p. 105.

[6]John White, *Parents in Pain*. Downers Grove, IL: InterVarsity Press, 1979, p. 105.

[7]White, p. 106.

[8]Howard G. Hendricks, *Heaven Help the Home!* Wheaton, IL: Victor Books, 1973, p. 29.

Discussion Questions

1. Think back to your own adolescence. What are some of your most pleasant and painful memories of being a teenager?

2. What is the strongest emotion that you experience as a parent of a teenager?

3. The author states, "For a teenager to successfully complete the pilgrimage from dependence to independence, he must debond from his parents." What is the most difficult part of the debonding phase for you as a parent?

4. How do you cope with the ungratefulness of your teens?

5. The author states that feelings of anger toward the teenager are normal, but actions of anger are wrong. What do you think about that statement?

6. How would you counsel a parent whose teenager is in serious trouble and is blaming himself for the failure?

7. Finish the statement, "I feel most inadequate as a parent when

_____

_____ ."

8. The author states that "all family relationships are based on the quality of your relationship with God." How have you seen this to be true or false?

9. Give examples of how the lack of closeness between a husband and wife can have a negative effect on the rearing of teenagers.

10. After reading this chapter and evaluating myself, one thing I will change to improve my parenting is ...

CHAPTER 2

"It's Different Now!"

Think back to your teenage years. What kind of feelings do you remember? Can you recall the first sexual awakenings of your body? Were you frightened by these awakenings? Did you feel excited or guilty?

How did you feel about your physical appearance? Did you mature early or late? Were you teased about your appearance? Did you have doubts about the sexual development of your body? Were you too tall or too short? Too fat or too skinny? Did you worry about your poor complexion? Do you remember strong feelings of self-doubt and self-hate?

How did you feel about strong sexual urges? Did you daydream about your own sexual adequacy? Did you wonder if you were becoming obsessed by sex? Were you confused about the issue of masturbation?

Most of us can identify with many of the above dilemmas of adolescence. For some, the pain was almost unbearable. For others, the adolescent years were much smoother. One thing we can all agree on is that it is not easy to be a teenager.

My adolescence was filled with much self-doubt and confusion. I was confused by a body that had sexual urges when I knew that acting out those urges was wrong. I continually questioned whether I was attractive to the opposite sex. I can vividly remember my first romance as a freshman in high school. I was elated because for the first time a girl that I liked, liked me. I was "in love." What a feeling! However, this first love did not last long. I soon began to notice that the girl of my dreams was interested in another boy in the youth group. I will never forget the feelings of rejection and low self-esteem I felt over the demise of my first romance. I can remember standing in front of the mirror and trying to decide if my looks were changing—if I was becoming ugly.

I characterized my adolescence as one of many self-doubts. I attended four different high schools in three years. I felt like I was on a treadmill, always trying to prove myself and gain acceptance of a new peer group. While I do remember a lot of good times during my teen years, *I would not want to go through adolescence again.*

It is surprising how quickly we forget the strong emotions of our adolescence. Perhaps it is because of the pain associated with that time in our life. Whatever the reason, the consequences are that we fail to be sensitive enough to what our teenagers are going through. We have a difficult time really putting ourselves in their shoes. Scripture says, "Don't just think about your own affairs, but be interested in others, too, and in what they are doing" (Philippians 2:4, *Living Bible).* We are to try to see things from another person's point of view. Be interested or sensitive to what they are experiencing.

Many times we fail to do this with our teenagers. We remember only that which is convenient for us to remember about our adolescence. This results in poor communication. The more we can remember about our own adolescence the more sensitive we can be to our own teenagers. Our teenagers are growing up in a different world than we experienced. Many things have changed.

A significant change is that puberty, that period when a person is first capable of reproducing sexually, comes much earlier than it once did. "In the United States—where children mature up to a year earlier than in European countries—the average age at first menstruation has declined from 14.2 in 1900 to about 12.45 today."[1] The prob-

Area	What It Was Like in My Teenage Years	Differences My Teenager Faces Today
Sex and Morality		
Value System		
Intergenerational Relationships		
Information		
Divorce/Single-Parent Families		
World Situation		
Depression and Suicide		
Pace of Society		
Finances		
Instant Solutions		

Figure 2-1. Then and Now

lem is that children's emotions are not maturing as fast as their bodies. There is no indication that those entering puberty at an early age are as mature emotionally as they are physically.

To help you get a grasp on "What it's like to be them" in this decade, take a brief break from your reading and fill out the "Differences" chart above. Go through each area listed, remembering what it was like when you were a teenager and what differences your teenager faces right now. Try to get a sense of what it is like for teenagers today.

As you reflect on the kind of world your teenager faces today, if you are like me, you felt yourself becoming tense. This is because adolescents of today really are growing up in a pressure cooker situation. An example is depression and suicide. Suicide is now the second leading cause of death among teenagers. According to a *U.S.A. Today* report, the death rate for people aged 15 to 24 has risen, while the rate for all other age groups has steadily declined. There's a common cause of it all—stress, says Michael Greenberg, a Rutgers University researcher studying violent teen deaths.[2]

Your teenagers also face unprecedented pressure in the area of sex and morality. According to Josh McDowell and Dick Day in their excellent book, *Why Wait*, "by age twenty, 81 percent of today's unmarried males and 67 percent of today's unmarried females have had sexual intercourse."[3]

The pressure to be sexually active is enormous. Our daughters have said that with the "in groups" in high school, you are just expected to be sexually active.

The value system that our teenagers are growing up in seems to be one of a focus on materialism and pleasure. With the tremendous impact of the TV, our teens are victims of the "You can have it all" message. This is the opposite of the message of God's Word to "be rich in good works" (1 Timothy 6:18).

The trend toward mobility continues in our country. A result is that we continue to depend less on those extended family and intergenerational relationships that helped generations past feel anchored and able to pass on family values. A study by Dr. H. Stephen Glenn in his booklet, *Developing Capable Young People*, shows significant interaction between family members down from 3 to 4 hours a day in 1930 to 14 1/2 minutes today.[4]

Our children are faced with a blast of information that would have been unimaginable to most of us in our generation. Just the knowledge of the vast amounts of information that our teens will be confronted with during their lifetime is enough to produce significant amounts of stress.

The amount of children living in single parent families continue to increase. Divorce has a major impact on the lives of teens. "A reader's survey of *Children and Teens today* asked, 'What do you see as the major stress/problems facing today's teenagers?' The response of 72.4 percent was: 'Problems arising from parental divorce/remarriage.'"[5]

Being reared in the nuclear age gives our teens great concern. Many believe that all will end up soon in a nuclear war, they find little reason for putting a great deal of effort into life goals.

The pace of our society is certainly not slowing. Our country continues to lead the world in frantic pace to do more, have more, and be more. Teens feel the pressure of that "hurry up through life" syndrome that affects all of us. There is very little time to "smell the roses," when most people are "going for the gold."

Generally speaking, teens have more money than we did when we were that age. Our teens' peer world pressures them to have at least average teen affluence. There is a price to be paid for this, as many teens crowd their already full schedules to overflowing to maintain the teen standard. Business has seen the tremendous potential for profit and competes fiercely for a share of teen money.

We are known as an "Instant Solution" society. If you're hungry and don't have time to fix dinner, you either stop at a fast food restaurant or pick up a TV dinner. If something goes wrong with an appliance, you call a repairman. There are gadgets to take care of about everything and pills to take care of our headaches when the gadgets don't work. The problem is that we take our instant solutions and quick fixes into other areas of life. We want solid family relationships with only a minimal amount of time spent in family time and one-on-one relationships. Our children have grown up with TV, which always solves interrelational problems in a half hour with minimal pain and consequences. Even your social life can be enhanced by using the right toothpaste. Unfortunately our teens are learning to expect instant solutions in many areas of life and avoid the discipline that it takes to make lasting solutions.

Aren't you glad that you don't have to face going through adolescence today? Well, that's the good news! The bad news, however, is that while we do not directly experience teenage traumas, we will be affected with some of the old feelings, as well as nervousness, as we help direct our children through those turbulent years.

As parents we can help our teenagers cope with the struggles of adolescence by assisting them in the three tasks of adolescence. These tasks, which every teenager must face, are self-identity, independence, and vocation.

Self-Identity

One of the greatest tasks of adolescence is for a teenager to achieve self-identity. He must be able to establish an identity of his own apart from his family. He must arrive at a real sense of who he is and feel good about himself. Erik H. Erikson, in his famous work on the stages of man, sees this as the most important task of adolescence. If a teenager does not develop a strong sense of self-identity during the teenage years, then it will be difficult for him to become intimate with others.[6] An intimate marriage will be impossible to achieve without first gaining self-identity. The next chapter will deal specifically on how you can help your teen in his pilgrimage toward solid self-identity.

Independence

Along with your teenager's search for self-identity comes his declaration of independence. He is no longer simply a part of your family, but is striving to make a name for himself—to be independent of you. In the previous chapter, we talked about this search for independence or the "debonding" process and the friction it causes in the family. In Chapter 4 I will give suggestions on how you can let go as you help your teenager move toward independence.

Vocation

The third great task of adolescence is for a teenager to move toward a meaningful vocation. One of the greatest needs of man, according to Maslow, creator of a hierarchy of human needs, is that of self-actualization. I define self-actualization as the ability to achieve the potential that God has placed in each one of us for the purpose of serving Him on earth. In Chapter 4, we will look at some ways to help your teen find his God-given gifts and use them in meaningful employment.

[1]*Psychology Today,* February, 1979, p. 45.

[2]*U.S.A. Today,* November 11, 1987, pp. 1A, 2A.

[3]Josh McDowell and Dick Day, *Why Wait?* San Bernardino, CA: Here's Life Publishers, 1987, p. 21.

[4]H. Stephen Glenn and Joel W. Warner, *Developing Capable Young People.* Hurst, TX: Humansphere, Inc.

[5]McDowell and Day, p. 35.

[6]Erik Erikson, *Identity and the Life Cycle.* New York: Norton, 1980.

Discussion Questions

1. Think back to your teenage years. Was your adolescence happy or unhappy? Share some of the feelings you experienced.

2. Finish the statement, "If I were to live my adolescence over again, I would _____."

3. What has it been convenient for you to forget about your adolescence?

4. Of the ten areas on the "Then and Now" activity, which one is most different than when you were growing up?

5. Which difference from the "Then and Now" activity do you see as most difficult for your teenager?

6. What difference concerns you most?

7. Share something about your teenager's search for his/her self-identity.

8. In what ways is your teenagers showing his/her need for independence?

9. What "gifts" has God given your children and how would you visualize them using those gifts in an occupation?

10. After reading this chapter, one thing I will do to better understand my teenagers' world is . . .

CHAPTER 3

"Mirror, Mirror on the Wall, Who Am I?"

Parents' Part of the Picture

We all remember the fairy tale of Snow White. The wicked queen who would stand in front of the mirror and say, "Mirror, mirror on the wall/Who's the fairest of them all?" In a sense all teenagers stand in front of that mirror daily and say, "Mirror, mirror on the wall, Who am I?" From that mirror there is no clear voice, but there are many reflections about who they are. They put these reflections together for a picture of themselves. Before we examine this mirror, let's first look at your own struggle for self-identity when you were an adolescent.

For most of us our teenage years were a constant search for who we really were. There was that nagging sense inside that we could no longer be an extension of our families and that the question of who we were must be answered before we could move on to the responsibilities of forming intimate relationships outside of the family and finding a meaningful occupation.

As we tried to answer the question, "Who am I?" most of us were on overload from our confused thoughts and feelings and often contradicting information about ourselves from peers, parents, and other significant adults. To get in touch with the struggle that your teen is now facing in working out his self-identity, answer the following open-ended questions about your own struggle in adolescence.

—I can remember feeling ...

—I felt most down on myself when ...

—I felt confident when ...

—One thing my parents did that helped me feel good about myself was ...

—One thing my parents did that did not enhance my self-esteem was ...

—I started coming to grips with who I really was when ...

Were you able to recapture some of those old feelings? If so, you have a sense of what your teenager is currently going through. The next time your daughter or son heads for school dressed in an outrageous outfit, remember they are trying to answer the question, "Who am I?" When your teenager drives you crazy by his moods, or "multiple personalities," it might help to think, "He is right on track," trying to figure out who he is.

Erik H. Erikson, in his famous work on the stages of man, sees this as the most important task of adolescence. If a teenager does not develop a strong sense of self-identity during the teenage years, then it will be difficult to achieve without first gaining a secure self-identity.

When teens are involved in such a chaotic search for who they are, it is normal for them to have periods of doubt accompanied by low self-esteem.

One study of seven thousand high school students reported by Merton Strommen in *Five Cries of Youth* found that the single most troublesome concern for teenagers was the feeling of self-hatred! "One of every five of these students reported severe problems with their self-esteem, and these were church youth! They reported feelings of failure, alienation, loneliness, lack of self-confidence, low self-regard and even thoughts of suicide! In short they weren't satisfied with their own identity."[1]

Often our teen's times of low self-esteem are easily recognized because these "down times" produce conflict in the home. There are other times when low self-esteem is difficult to detect because it is well hidden.

Some friends of ours told us about some deep-seated feelings of low self-esteem that they discovered in their teenage daughter. The incident occurred during a family time. Each person was answering questions that had been written on index cards. One of the questions was, "What do you contribute to this family, and how do you feel about it?" When it came time for the teenage daughter to respond she cried, "Nothing. I do not contribute anything to this family."

The entire family quickly came to her aid, reaffirming the fact that she was an important part of the family and contributed in many positive ways. The parents, however, were caught by surprise. They had no idea she was dealing with such intense feelings of self-hate. This can happen to any of us. Our teens are adept at hiding painful feelings when they feel it is to their advantage. We must assume that even though our teenagers have cool exteriors, that many times there could be a real battle for self-identity going on inside.

As we have seen, your teen's journey through adolescence is bound to lower his self-esteem. There will be certain things your teenager does not like about himself. It may be his physical appearance, his interaction with the opposite sex, his lack of achievement in areas he feels are important. It may be his lack of understanding of his own great emotional mood swings. It may be his lack of ability to get along with other members of the family. Whatever the cause, you can be assured that his self-esteem at times will be very low.

Conflict is inevitable with a teen with lowered self-esteem, with the need to establish his own self-identity and a need to challenge parental authority and values. If we withdraw our love and approval from our teens, however, their self-esteem is lowered yet another notch. The sad result is that a teen who loses parental approval will seek approval from his peer group.

With the search for self-identity comes a wide range of strong emotions. These new strong feelings are not understood by your teens, so how can they possibly explain them to you? Many will not even try. Most will feel embarrassed because they cannot put their feelings into words. It is helpful if we talk to our teens about their feelings. We should never try to drag explanations about their feelings from them. We need to assure them that it's normal for them to have strong feelings that are different to understand and express. We should not feel personally insulted if our teens choose not to share their feelings with us.

With the turbulent emotions can come drastic mood changes. One minute your teen can be ecstatic about life; the next minute, surly and angry at almost everything. One day your teen can be fiercely independent; the next day wanting to be pampered like a child.

As your teenagers grow older, and move toward a stronger self-identity, their feelings will come more in balance with their thinking. Figure 3-1 shows how this occurs. In early adolescence feelings dominate with the balance between feelings and thinking not coming until the ages of 16-19. For you parents that are concerned about the strong emotions and mood changes, *hang on.* God's timetable says, "not yet."

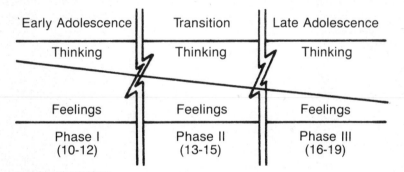

Early Adolescence	Transition	Late Adolescence
Thinking	Thinking	Thinking
Feelings	Feelings	Feelings
Phase I (10-12)	Phase II (13-15)	Phase III (16-19)

Figure 3-1. The Balance Between Thinking and Feeling

Bruce Narramore gives five areas in which our teenagers want to know who they are: (1) "Our teenagers want to know who they are physically." They want their bodies to be acceptable, to reach their potential. (2) "Our teenagers want to know who they are sexually." They want to understand what is going on in their bodies. They want to know if they will be acceptable to the opposite sex. (3) "Teenagers also need to know who they are socially." They want to explore their relationships with others, so they can find out where they fit. They want to know who will accept them. (4) "Our teenagers want to investigate their education and vocational identity." They want to answer the question, "What am I going to accomplish with my life?" (5) "Teenagers want to know their spiritual identity." They want to know that God loves and accepts them unconditionally. They want to know how they fit into God's plan, and how they can know God's will in their life.[2]

How Can We Help?

By now you are probably asking, "Is there anything we as parents can do to help our teenagers in the area of self-esteem? What can we do to help them establish that self-identity and develop good feelings about themselves?" I have good and bad news for you. The good news is, we can do some things to help our teens develop self-identity and feel good about themselves. The bad news is, there's a limit to what we can do. The ultimate responsibility for self-esteem comes from the teen himself and his relationship with God. We all have to be responsible to God for ourselves. It is all too tempting to blame ourselves for our children's problems. Often I hear parents say, "If I had been a better parent," or "If I had been more affirming," etc. But the fact is we all have to overcome some self-esteem lowering experiences from our homes. There is no way we can parent in such a way that our children will be assured of positive self-esteem. This is because we are all imperfect human beings. The most we can do is lay a foundation for our children to develop positive feelings about themselves.

It is not unusual to attempt to lay a sound foundation and still have to watch our children go through tremendous self-esteem struggles. Such was the case with our youngest child, Bridget. For years Janet and I were concerned with her low self-esteem. We worried about what would happen when she got to high school. Shortly after Bridget started her ninth-grade year some of our worst expectations began to happen. We saw her start associating with teens who had problems. We observed the downward spiral as we watched her self-reproach drag her down. The inevitable experimenting with drugs came. We felt helpless as parents.

The only thing Janet and I could do at this point was trust God and Bridget's future and pray diligently for her. An amazing thing happened at the beginning of her sophomore year. She immediately developed a complete new group of friends—friends who were achievers and had values similar to the families. We watched in amazement as she began to feel better about herself. That self-hatred started to fade. The trend continued, and as we look at her now as a delightful remarkably confident senior in high school, we can only thank God. It was nothing we did. It was Bridget taking responsibility for her relationship with God and her own life.

The mirror on the next page will help you summarize how our teenagers form their self-identity and where you as parents fit into the picture.

Reflections From God

The first and most important reflection in your child's life is the reflection from God's viewpoint. Teenagers need to understand the full impact of being precious children of God (John 1:12), adopted into His family with full rights as children of the king (Galatians 4:5). They need to know that God's love is so great for them that He sent His Son so they could learn of that great love (John 3:16). Teenagers need to know that they are unconditionally loved and forgiven by God. What a tremendous self-esteem builder to know that we are valued as special children of our heavenly Father.

Physical Appearance and Athletic Ability

Teenagers take careful notice of whether they are seen as attractive by their peers. Physical appearance and athletic ability affect their self-esteem significantly during the teenage years. The mirror on the wall sometimes judges them harshly during this time.

Competence

Teenagers are asking the mirror on the wall, "Am I competent?" This important question has to do with how well

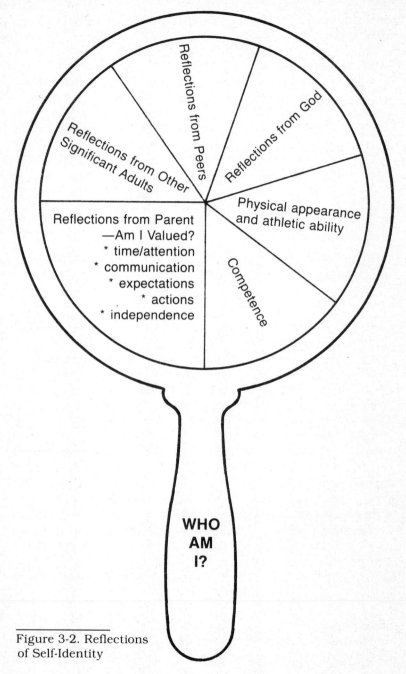

Reflections from Peers

Reflections from God

Reflections from Other Significant Adults

Physical appearance and athletic ability

Reflections from Parent
—Am I Valued?
* time/attention
* communication
* expectations
* actions
* independence

Competence

**WHO
AM
I?**

Figure 3-2. Reflections
of Self-Identity

they do at schoolwork and such areas that their peers, parents, and other significant adults see as important.

Reflections From Peers

A strong influence on how teenagers feel about themselves is input about themselves they receive from peers. This input can be confusing, because peers are often unreliable evaluators of what makes a human being valuable.

Reflections From Other Significant Adults

At times it may not seem like our teens really care what other adults think of them, but in reality they do. They receive many important reflections from adults other than their mother and father—relatives, family friends, bosses, teachers, etc. What these people think of them has a large impact on how teens think of themselves.

Reflections From Parents

The reflections parents give to teenagers about themselves has a tremendous impact on their self-image. The parents' voice from the mirror comes loud and clear and it echoes for years to come. The major question it is answering for teenagers is, "Am I valued?" The greatest thing a parent can do for his teenager's self-esteem is truly value to him in a way that the adolescent *feels* valued. There are five major areas in which positive reflections from parents can help a teenager feel valued.

Time/attention. Spending time and focusing attention on teenagers is a tangible way they measure whether or not they are valued by parents. Now I can hear some of you saying, "But they don't want my time and attention. They fight it." Not so! They do want *some* of our time and *some* of our attention, but unfortunately for us, they want it on their terms. The when and how much is dictated by their whims. It may seem unfair, but it is a fact. I have to watch Bridget for clues on when she wants my time and attention. Out of the blue she will say, "Dad, let's go to breakfast." It seems that she always asks at inconvenient times. I often initially think, "no way," but almost always I will say yes when I've had time to reflect. I know that there are not many of these times left, and I want her to feel valued.

Communication. Our teenagers feel valued when we take time to listen to them and share ourselves with them. Communication with teenagers, I'll admit, takes lots of patience and again it is often on their terms and turf. Talking to them as valued friends goes far in terms of building their self-esteem.

Expectations. What we expect from our teens significantly influences whether they feel valued or believe they are a possession to live out our wishes for their life. Expecting too much from our teenagers or expecting them to live out our dreams and not their own create low self-esteem. Our children really do want to please us, but if they feel they are continually falling short of what we want for them, their self-esteem will be undermined.

Actions. How we treat our teens reflects to them how much they are valued. Questions we should ask ourselves are: Do we affirm our teenagers on a regular basis? Does the way we discipline them reflect to them that they are valued? Does our attitude tell them that they are valued?

Independence. When we allow our teenagers progressively more responsibility and independence, it says to them that they are competent, valued persons. Allowing our teens to surge toward independence shows that we have confidence in them. It is reasonable to assume that if we show confidence in them that this will help them to become more confident in themselves.

If we can polish these parental reflections, we will be making a significant contribution to our teenagers' search for "who they are." Remember, as painful as it is to watch our children struggle in their development of self-identity, it is a necessary part of the development each person must face on his way to maturity.

---

[1]Merton Strommen, *Five Cries of Youth.* New York: Harper and Row, 1974.
[2]Bruce Narramore, *Adolescence Is Not an Illness.* Old Tappan, NJ: Revell, 1980, pp. 40, 41.

Discussion Questions

1. Choose one of the open-ended questions on page 35 and share your answer with the group.

2. Have you seen any signs of self-hatred in your teenager? How did *you* feel?

3. What signs indicate your teenager is feeling down on himself?

4. Where on the scale of thinking/feeling (page 37) is your teenager right now?

5. On a scale of 1-10, with ten being perfect, how would you rate your teenager in his development of self-identity?

6. Bruce Narramore gives five areas in which our teenagers want to know who they are. In which area is your teenager struggling the most right now?

7. What do you usually do when you see your teenager struggling with his self-esteem?

8. When your teenager faces the mirror on the wall, which reflection influences his view of himself most?

9. Which of the parental reflections do you need to "polish"?

10. Choose one thing you will do to help your teenager in his struggle to answer, "Who am I?"

CHAPTER 4

"I Don't Need You Anymore"

A Job Well Done?

"I don't need you anymore."

These should be wonderful words for us to hear. After all, haven't we worked hard to launch our teenagers into the world as competent Christian individuals? Shouldn't we have the kind of good feelings that accompany the completion of significant long-term goals in our lives?

Despite the many "shoulds," the fact remains that our feelings are often ambivalent when it comes to our teenagers' growing independence. On one hand, we are glad that they are showing signs of maturity and an ability to face the world on their own. On the other hand, we experience feelings of loss as we become aware that we will not be needed like we once were. The loss is especially significant if our self-esteem has been too closely associated with our teens needing us.

In addition to the feelings of loss, there are the feelings of uncertainty about how well our teenagers will function in the cruel, hard world. We would like to protect them from some of the hurts they are sure to face. In all, the launching of our teenagers is a bittersweet experience of conflicting emotions on the part of both parents and adolescents.

Let Me Go—Sometimes

The conflicting emotions our teenagers face are caused by the tension between a need to feel independent and a need to feel dependent and secure. While our teenagers know they must debond, there is still that strong attraction because of the bonding years. The ambivalent feelings of our teenagers often cause friction and confuse parents who see their adolescent demand independence one day and want to be taken care of the next.

Much of this friction comes because our teens must convince themselves that they no longer need us. Friction between a teenager and his parents makes the separation a little easier.

We must realize that some faultfindings, talking back, questioning, and anger is part of the normal breaking away process. I realize how hard it is not to take some of these affronts personally! After all, parents have feelings too! We must keep reminding ourselves that we really are making a significant impact on their life, despite how we sometimes feel at the moment.

Parents do have a significant impact on the lives of their teenagers, as Jay Kesler points out.

> From a scientific viewpoint, we are of much greater influence as parents than we might have thought. A few years ago, Youth for Christ International commissioned a study of the value systems and authority figures in the lives of America's high school students. Somewhat to our surprise, parents ranked a very close second to peer's influence. In areas of values, teens agreed with their parents in almost everything from political persuasion to morals. This is why the 18-year-old vote has not affected our political structure to any appreciable degree. Apparently, de-parenting is not as risky as it seems. Parents continue to make an impact on the essential nature of their children.

It's good to remember that much of our teens' rebellious behavior helps them defend themselves against the pain they feel when venturing into the unknown of the grownup world.

There is often friction over the loss of family time as teenagers stretch toward independence. They no longer seem to need that cozy family feeling that doing things with the family once produced. This in itself can be threatening, especially if you have done a lot together as a family.

Loss of family time bothered Janet and I. When the children were young we did lots of things together as a family. We were tempted to try to maintain the same type of family togetherness that we had during those early years. However, we knew this would only make matters worse. We gradually settled for less family time than we really desired.

Jay Kesler introduces us to one of the real issues in allowing our teenagers to debond—balance.

> Rather than accept the inevitable erosion of family time by conflicting schedules and individual interests, parents begin to tighten down the screws. Somehow we feel that responsibility for our family means that we must dictate every moment and give account for every activity of every member of our family. This is impossible as our kid reaches teen age. It is also undesirable. We need to be cultivating the kind of relationship that is made of mutual trust. How, for instance, can a husband be sure his wife is faithful while he is at work? Their relationship insures it.[2]

A High Wire Balancing Act

How do we know when we are allowing our teenagers enough freedom or too much freedom? According to our teenagers, it seems like we *never* allow them enough freedom. Trying to find the right balance is like attempting to walk a high wire in a circus. There is danger in leaning too far in either direction. There is no exact formula to help us balance the area of our teen's independence. We can, however, evaluate whether our approach is too slow—too tight, too fast—too loose, or not too slow—not too fast—just about right.

Too Slow—Too Tight
Some families tend to release their children too slowly and hold too tight a rein on them in the process. Parents in these families have a need to keep their children dependent upon them. In some cases it's a reluctance to give up those

close family feelings. In other cases it's a need to be needed. With other parents it is a fear of what might happen to their teens once they are on their own.

There is nothing more pathetic than a young person who has been kept dependent by his parents. When I was taking basic training at Fort Ord, California, we had a recruit in our platoon named Norris. Norris was from a wealthy east coast family. While the rest of us were reading the funnies, Norris would be reading the stock market report, finding out how much his family had made that day. Norris was a brilliant young man. Intellectually few of us could compete with him. On a practical level, however, Norris could barely tie his shoes. He had been kept dependent all of his life by a doting mother and a protective nurse. They had done everything for him.

I will always be able to visualize some of Norris' traumas in basic training. For example, we would "fall out" for reveille each morning at 5:30. Each person in our platoon would be standing at rigid attention—all, that is, except Norris. We would hear the slam of the barrack door and the pitter patter of Norris's combat boots. The curiosity would become too much for me, and I would sneak a look at Norris. The risk was always worth it. There Norris would be with the bottom of his canteen sticking straight up in the air, his boots untied, or an important part of the uniform missing. Poor Norris found it impossible to even get dressed. On the target range Norris would often hit the bull's-eye—but not his own. When Norris was learning to toss a hand grenade, he was completely engulfed by people who were committed to his not blowing up himself or everyone else. Norris was a mess! Why? Because his parents kept him dependent. I expect Norris has suffered all his life.

This is an extreme case, but it is surprising how many well-meaning parents subtly pressure their children to remain dependent, sometimes without consciously recognizing what they are doing.

Here is a series of questions you can ask yourself to evaluate if you lean towards "too slow—too tight."

—Do you allow your teenager to face the consequences in his/her life or do you rescue him/her?

—Do you see independence as a positive characteristic in your teenager's life?

—Do you allow your teenager an increasing amount of responsibility in his/her life in the areas of curfew, leisure time, friends, vocation, etc.?

—Are you changing your role from authority and protector to friend and guide?

—Do you allow a *decreasing* amount of mandatory family time?

"No" answers in the above areas indicate a tendency towards "too slow—too tight" in allowing your teenager to become independent.

Too Fast—Too Loose

Parents can also get out of balance by being too fast with freedom and too loose in their rules and regulations. In fact, the weight of imbalance in our society today is towards giving teenagers too much independence at too early an age. A contributing factor to this phenomenon is the significant number of adolescents living in single parent homes. Add to this the teenagers who grow up in homes where both parents work. Many parents are simply not around much to supervise their teens.

What many parents do not realize is that this freedom can be harmful to their teenagers. Child development psychologist Erik Erikson has developed a model where children go through predictable stages on the way to maturity. He concludes that if teenagers are given freedom and responsibility beyond their stage, they can suffer emotional and social damage.

Tony Campolo, chairman of the sociology department at Eastern College in St. Davids, Pennsylvania, speaks of this problem in an article in YOUTHWORKER magazine. Campolo says, of junior highers,

> Very few of today's authority figures keep them from what they want to do, but these early adolescents cannot exercise their freedom without inordinate fear and trepidation. Studies show, consequently, that high school graduates looking back on their junior high years wish their parents had asked more questions of them and exercised more restraints on their behavior. Such declarations seem strange by those

who, during junior high, seemed to be constantly trying to get parents off their backs. But studies indicate that what junior highers say they want, is not what they actually desire.[3]

I have watched parents give in to the demands for freedom that their teenagers say they want. Often teenagers see such permissiveness as a lack of caring and love rather than concern. Not too long ago, Bridget confronted us with her belief that we were not strict enough with her curfew. We assumed since Bridget was responsible about being where she said she would be and coming home at a reasonable time that she would feel good about us letting her set her own hours. She was interpreting our actions as not caring rather than as a compliment on her responsibility. She was saying to us, "Inside I know I am not ready for the freedom you are giving me. It scares me."

I have recently been concerned about a Christian family who's daughter has been rebelling. They hung in there for a while, but then they completely gave up. The teenage girl comes and goes as she wishes and does what she wants. While outwardly demanding all this freedom, I believe inside she really wants the security of her parents' restraints. I think she will someday say, "You didn't care." I have often heard teenagers say, "My parents knew what I was doing and didn't even care enough to make me stop." Tough love says, "I love you too much to let you self-destruct."

Here is a series of questions you can ask yourself to evaluate if you lean towards "Too fast—too loose."

—Do you give your teenager unrestricted or almost unrestricted freedom in terms of activities and curfew?

—Do you follow through with discipline when your teenager disobeys?

—Do you ask your teenager to be available for some family time?

—Do you spend some personal time each week asking your teenager questions about what's going on—in school, at work, with friends, and with activities?

—Do you stand strong on your convictions when your teen rebels, or do you give in to his demands?

A "yes" answer to the first question and "no" answers to

the following four questions indicate a tendency towards "too fast—too loose" in allowing your teenager to become independent.

Not Too Slow—Not Too Fast—Just About Right

As parents of teenagers, we all want to be "just about right" in the area of our children's independence. If you answered most of the questions in a positive direction, then you probably have developed a good balance toward releasing your teenager toward independence. Figure 4-1 is a scale to help you locate approximately where you think you are in balancing the debonding task you face with your teenager. Below is a scale to rate whether your adolescent is trying to move toward independence too slowly, too quickly, or just about right. These scales could make good discussion starters for you and your teens. Have them rate you and themselves. Then discuss the difference between your ratings and their ratings.

Circle the number that best indicates how you believe you are releasing your teenager and how your teenager is releasing himself.

	Too slow			Just About Right					Too Fast	
Parent 1	1	2	3	4	5	6	7	8	9	10
Parent 2	1	2	3	4	5	6	7	8	9	10
Teen 1	1	2	3	4	5	6	7	8	9	10
Teen 2	1	2	3	4	5	6	7	8	9	10

One thing I will do to better balance this area of my parenting is:

_____

_____

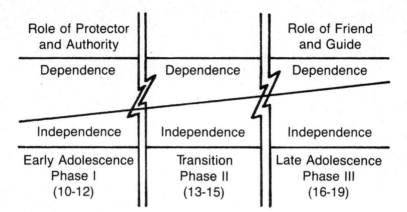

Role of Protector and Authority	Role of Friend and Guide
Dependence	Dependence	Dependence
Independence	Independence	Independence
Early Adolescence Phase I (10-12)	Transition Phase II (13-15)	Late Adolescence Phase III (16-19)

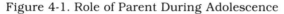

Figure 4-1. Role of Parent During Adolescence

Helping Our Teenagers Become Independent

In three vital areas, you can make a significant impact in your teenager's pilgrimage toward independence.

Allowing Your Teenager to Suffer Consequences

It is natural for us to want to protect our teenagers from pain, but pain is a part of the maturing process. James says, "Consider it all joy, my brethren, when you encounter various trials, knowing that the testing of your faith produces endurance. And let endurance have its perfect result, that you may be perfect and complete, lacking in nothing" (James 1:2-4).

Some of the trials that come into our teenagers' lives will be produced by their own unwise actions. Other will be as a result of external circumstances. We should never interfere with God's plan to build maturity in our teens as a result of trials. Let me hasten to say that sometimes we do interfere in times of what we consider to be spiritual danger. I believe that is always appropriate. God does not expect us to allow our teenagers to commit spiritual suicide. Many times we step in too soon and do not allow our teens to suffer the natural consequences of their actions. Our teens will mature as they learn from their mistakes. We can help as we wipe away the tears after the "skinned knees." We should never project the attitude, "I told you so," but always be sensitive to the lessons God is teaching them in their young lives.

Dean Pense, senior pastor of a church in which we worked together, told me the story of his teenage son who just *had* to have a high-performance, gas-guzzling car. Dean explained all the pitfalls of such a car to his son, but the counsel fell on deaf ears. Instead of saying no to his son's request Dean said, "It's your decision and your money." The expensive lesson started immediately. Six months later his son traded the car in on a smaller, more efficient car at considerable financial loss. There was never a word said by Dean about the incident, but his son had learned a valuable lesson. Dean had allowed him to fail and reap the consequences. If Dean had stepped in and denied his son's request, his teenager would not have learned a valuable lesson from life. It is hard to stand by and see our teenagers lose money or get burned by relationships, but it produces "completeness" or maturity in the end.

Change Your Role to Friend and Guide

When our children are young our role as parent is much more of protector and authority. As our teenagers stretch for independence we must change our role to a friend and guide. The role of a strict authoritarian who tells them what to do is no longer the most productive style. I realize that we still are an authority in their lives, and that there are still plenty of direct orders, but our style needs to be changing. This change includes giving our teens the same tone of voice and respect in our communication that we do a good friend. It is easier for them to respond to us when we have such an attitude. Our counsel to them needs to be more indirect. We need to suggest options to them and let them make the decisions. Your teenager's mental development, especially during late adolescence (16-19), enables him to make more and more wise decisions. It's good for us to remember that they are only a few years away from making their decisions with little or no help from us. They need lots of practice in the security of our home. We want to help our children "develop the ability to learn from the past, live in the present, and move toward the future."[4]

Trust That God Is Active in Your Teenager's Life

A good friend, Carmella Gillons, once told me, "I finally had to realize that I could not be the Holy Spirit in my teenager's life. That was God's job and I had to allow Him to do His work."

I have thought a lot about that insight, and I believe it is something all parents need to hear. God, through His Holy Spirit, will work His will in our children's lives. We simply need to trust God to work in our teenager's lives in the same way He works in ours.

[1]Jay Kesler, *Too Big to Spank*. Ventura, CA: Regal, 1978, p. 39.
[2]Kesler, p. 17.
[3]Tony Campolo, "Too Old Too Soon—the New Junior Higher," *Youthworker*, Vol. IV, No. 1, p. 21.
[4]James R. Oraker and Char Meredith, *Almost Grown*. New York: Harper and Row, 1980, p. 81.

Discussion Questions

1. What is the first thing that comes into your mind when you hear "I don't need you anymore" from your teenager? How do you feel?

2. What are some conflicting emotions that you have when facing your teenager's independence?

3. What does your teenager do that shows he wants to be independent but still dependent at the same time?

4. How do you handle the loss of family time in your home? How is it working?

5. Where on the Dependence/Independence Scale did you rate yourself? Did you discover anything that surprised you?

6. Where on the Dependence/Independence Scale did you rate your teenager?

7. How well do you do in allowing your teenager to suffer the consequences of his actions?

8. How are you doing in the area of changing your role to friend and guide?

9. To what degree are you able to trust that God is active in your teenager's life?

10. What one thing will you change to help your teenager in his task of becoming independent?

Section Two

Building the Structure— Developing Skills

CHAPTER 5

How to Listen
So Your Teenager
Will Talk

"You never listen." How often has your teenager said this to you in the middle of a discussion? Our teenagers often accuse us of not listening and they are probably correct.

Poor listening skills seem to be a universal human dilemma. Lee Iacocca in his autobiography listed poor listening skills as the greatest problem with managers. Iacocca said that if there was a "Listening Institute" he would send all of his managers to it.

This chapter is a "listening institute" for the parents of teenagers. We all need to sharpen our listening skills. Often we developed poor listening skills in our homes when we were growing up. Our education did not help. There was no basic course in listening in high school, and no "Listening 101" in college. If we have a successful marriage, then we developed some listening skills out of necessity. But even these skills seem to diminish when we try to listen to our teenagers.

Control Talk

What goes on between parents and teenagers that makes listening so difficult? I believe a primary problem with parents is what I call "Control Talk." When we have conflict with teens we feel a need to control what is going on, so we mind read, lecture, demand, and scold in an attempt to be in control of the situation. If we are trying to control the conversation and our teenagers through control talk, then we are certainly not listening so our teenagers will talk.

What happens when we start our control talk is that our teenagers get immediately into a defensive mode, which I call "Anti-control Talk." The basic intent is to move up from control to out of control! Some might clam up and say nothing. Some might get very emotional and scream, "You never listen." Others might engage us in a no-win argument. Our control talk might have worked when our children were in the bonding stage, but it does not work with teenagers who are becoming independent. They will fight control talk as they do other restraints they see as a threat to their independence. As parents we must move from "control" type communication to "Straight Talk" (Chapter 6) and "Strategic Listening."

Definition of Listening

Listening is a commitment to *understand what another person feels, thinks, and wants.* This definition includes an attitude of, "I want to understand you." Listening is really one of the ultimate acts of love. It is an act of love because the person being listened to *feels* loved and the person who is listening is extending himself in the very difficult *work* of listening. James speaks of the importance of this work of love when he says, "Let every one be quick to hear, slow to speak and slow to anger. For the anger of man does not achieve the righteousness of God" (James 1:19, 20). In this chapter we are learning the Biblical precepts of being "quick to hear" and "slow to speak."

Three Obstacles to Listening

There are three obstacles that we must remove if we are going to truly listen to our teens. These are: judging, preparing, and lecturing. Notice that these are all "Control Talk" tactics.

Judging

It is impossible to hear what a person feels, thinks, and wants if we have already judged them. Judging means deciding in advance that the person is wrong before we have heard them out. It is often difficult for us to hear our teenagers out, but it is a necessary part of being a good listener. Proverbs 18:13 says, "He who gives an answer before he hears, It is folly and shame to him." Proverbs 13:10 gives us further admonition in this area, "Through presumption comes nothing but strife, But with those who receive counsel is wisdom."

Preparing

Another obstacle to listening is that we are preparing what we are going to say to our teenager while he is talking. It is obvious that we cannot listen while we are rehearsing what we are going to say next. It takes great discipline to listen and not to be preparing our defense.

Lecturing

I am an expert in this obstacle to listening. I love to lecture. I have so much wisdom to impart to my wayward-thinking teenager. The problem is, of course, that I cannot listen when I am lecturing and my teenager is totally unimpressed by expertise. Any type of lecturing on the part of us a parents is read by our teenagers as saying we have no interest in what they feel, think, or want. The book of Proverbs warns us against the danger of too many inappropriate words. "The one who guards his mouth, preserves his life; the one who opens wide his lips, comes to ruin" (Proverbs 13:3).

Strategic Listening

Strategic listening means that we have a strategy to our listening. This strategy includes the four listening posts of strategic listening and the three "A's" of strategic listening.

Four Listening Posts of Strategic Listening

Listening post 1—facts. When we listen strategically, we listen for facts. Facts are data. Facts are what we see and hear. It is easy for us to forget to listen for facts in a conflict situation and go directly to what we think, how we feel or what we want. For example, your teenage daughter was supposed to be in at 12:00 on Friday evening. This had been agreed upon. It is 1:15 a.m. and you are getting worried.

You're about to start making phone calls when your daughter bursts into the house. "I'm home, sorry I'm late," she says, and heads down the hall for her room.

You say, "Wait a minute—not so fast. You were supposed to be in at 12:00. You know you are supposed to call when you are late. How could you be so insensitive?"

In this conversation there are some missing facts. It is appropriate to show your teenager that you have been worried and upset, but until you have asked for the missing facts you have not really started listening. There are already two given facts—your teenager was to be in at 12:00 and it is now 1:15. Your teenager is late. What you don't know is what happened. A simple "What happened?" or "Why are you late?" will fill in the missing information. Your teenager may supply some relevant facts, such as, "We fell asleep while watching a video," or "We had car trouble." You may disagree that the facts are a reason for your teenager to be late—but now at least you are ready to move on to the next listening post, *beliefs.*

Listening post 2—beliefs. Beliefs are what we think. They are our interpretations of the data. They are our assumptions. It is important for you to listen for your teenager's beliefs—they are probably much different than yours. Two people can look at the same set of facts and arrive at different conclusions. In the case of the late daughter, she might say, "I didn't think you would care," or "You should trust me," or "Why do you always worry? You know I can take care of myself," or "I should be able to choose what time I come in." These are all beliefs—your teenager's way of looking at the situation. Once you have heard your teenager's beliefs, you can then discuss differences in what you believe and they believe. When you listen for beliefs, you will at least know where the basic differences lie.

Listening post 3—feelings. Often we neglect listening for one another's feelings. Feelings are our gut-level emotions and are often the most difficult to hear. For example, when your teenage daughter returns home late your innermost emotion is probably fear over her safety, but the emotion you are most apt to show is anger. You daughter might also cover her emotion of not being trusted by showing anger. It is especially difficult when we are emotional to listen to the feelings of our teenager, but it is important. Listening to the feelings of our teenagers without judging those feelings is one of the real keys to listening so our teenagers will talk. When someone is aware of and accepts our feelings, we feel loved and understood. When we feel understood and accepted, we are willing to risk even more.

Listening post 4—interests. Interest is what we want and need. Interest is what motivates or moves us to action. For example, in the continuing story of the daughter who was late, she might have simply wanted to continue having fun. Or she might have needed to feel independent, and by coming in late she was declaring that need to her mother. We need to listen intently for the wants and needs of our teenagers. This listening post is often the key to our conflict with them. Many times what our teenager wants and what we want are in conflict. For example, in the previous illustration, we might need to know that our teenager is safe. The need is in opposition to the daughter's need to be independent. However, the two needs can be negotiated once each person knows what they are. The very fact that our teens are moving toward independence means that there are going to be conflicting needs.

Use of the four listening posts will dramatically increase your ability to really hear your teenager. This is a skill area, however, that will take a lot of practice and discipline.

Three A's of Strategic Listening

By understanding the four listening posts, we know *what* to listen for. By learning to use the three A's of strategic listening, we know *how* to listen.

Acknowledging. We can acknowledge facts, beliefs, feelings and wants by reflecting back to our teenager in some way what he said or what we have perceived. In the case of the teenage daughter who said, "You should trust me," the parent could acknowledge the feeling, you are not necessarily agreeing that she *should* be feeling that way, only that she *is* feeling not trusted and that she has a right to her own feelings. By having her feelings acknowledged, the daughter now believes that the mother is at least trying to understand and will probably keep on talking about the situation. If the mother says, "What do you mean, we don't trust you? We give you all kinds of freedom," the daughter feels not listened to and the conversation will probably become unproductive.

In the same situation, the mother could acknowledge the daughter by responding to a want. "It seems from what you are saying that you want more freedom." Again the daughter will feel listened to and will probably keep on sharing her perspectives on the issue.

Asking. We can ask about facts, beliefs, feelings, and wants. By using questions such as what, how, when, and where we can clarify what the person is really saying. Asking is a powerful way of listening. Again, returning to our ongoing saga of the teenage girl, the mother could use this listening technique by asking the girl, "What am I doing that causes you to believe that you are not trusted?" or "What do you want changed that would help you feel more trusted?" Asking questions, using the four areas of the listening posts, helps focus your listening so that your teenager will give information that will help resolve issues.

Accepting. Accepting is not agreeing. You do not have to agree with your teenagers' beliefs, feelings, or wants to accept their right to their own beliefs, feelings, and wants. Often we do not understand how another person is feeling. Sometimes we wonder how they could possibly feel or think the way they do. Their feelings and thoughts are different than ours. This is especially true with teenagers. How could the teenage daughter feel not trusted because, "after all, we trust her in almost all areas." Nevertheless, the daughter at that moment is not *feeling* trusted. Right or wrong, the feeling is real and that is what you, as a parent, are accepting. Telling a person that their feelings are stupid or invalid simply crushes their spirit and eliminates any hope of further conversation. Discussing feelings, beliefs, and wants is appropriate, but only after your teenager feels that you are accepting his right to his personhood.

Conclusion

I have given you some helpful principles to increase your ability to listen to your teenager. These are simple basics that are difficult to apply. They are difficult because we are not used to being disciplined listeners. They are also difficult because we are human beings that always function somewhere beneath our ideals. If you, however, take some of the principles and use them some of the time, you are well on your way to becoming a *very good* listener. And remember, listening to teenagers is no piece of cake!

Discussion Questions

1. When I think about listening to my teenagers, I feel

   _____

2. The most difficult thing about listening to my teenager is

   _____

3. What indication is there that you use "control talk" and your teenagers use "anti-control talk"?

4. What do you think about the author's definition of listening?

5. Which obstacle to listening do you most often use? How does your teenager respond?

6. Which of the "listening posts" given by the author do you have the most difficult time using? Why?

7. What is your usual reaction when your teenager expresses strong negative emotions?

8. When do *you* feel most listened to?

9. Which of the three A's of strategic listening do you need to work on most?

10. I will do the following to become a better listener to my teenager:

CHAPTER 6

How to Talk So Your Teenager Will Listen

If I could really deliver on the implied promise of the title to this chapter, I could make a fortune. What parent wouldn't invest a fortune to learn to talk so their teenager would listen. There is no magic formula to guarantee that your teenager will listen no matter how skillfully you talk. There is a method, however, that will make it easier for you to talk to your teenager and make it easier for him to listen.

Straight Talk

How often have you wished that there was something you could do to get your message across? You need to confront your teenager, but you are afraid the confrontation will end up like many others—disastrous, with hurt feelings on both sides. For example, you have just got the word—your teenager has been deceitful. He told you he was going to spend the night at a friend's but failed to mention that he was going to a wild party. You are disappointed because you trusted your son and he took advantage. You are angry because he disobeyed clear-cut rules. Now you have to confront him and you are not looking forward to the scene.

How would you handle the situation? You will have to fill in the blanks here because each of us have different styles of handling confrontations. Most of us have trouble confronting in a constructive way. Some of us explode in anger. Others hold our anger inside and let it leak out in a passive-aggressive way, by looks or withholding affection.

Whatever your style of confrontation, straight talk can help you confront in a more effective manner. Straight talk helps us get a handle on the Biblical admonition in James 1:19, "be slow to speak." Straight talk enables us to think about what we are *feeling* and what we *want* and say it in such a way that our teenager is given maximum opportunity to really hear what we are saying.

To share my feelings with someone else I must, of course, be aware of what I am feeling. This has several benefits. Not only do I understand myself more fully, I also start becoming more sensitive to the feelings of my family. Of course, I must be aware of my feelings before I can communicate them to my teenager.

Awareness comes by allowing ourselves to feel (accepting our feelings as a gift from God) and by examining our feelings. Many times we concentrate on what we think so much that we fail to bring how we feel into balance. How often do you stop and think, "What is the feeling that I am experiencing right now?"

Feelings Are a Gift From God

We must first accept our feelings as a gift from God. It is not hard for most Christians to accept their positive feelings as a gift from God, but many people feel the negative feelings are directly from Satan.

God has gifted us with a full range of feelings, both positive and negative. These feelings are neither good nor bad. They have no morality. What we do with these feelings— our actions—can be good or bad. There is a difference, for example, between angry feelings and angry actions.

Jesus experienced the full range of feelings and did not sin. In Mark 3:1-5 we find the Pharisees watching Jesus in the synagogue to see if He would heal on the Sabbath. Jesus knew their thoughts and became *angry.* "And after looking around at them with anger, grieved at their hardness of heart, He said to the man, 'Stretch out your hand.' And he stretched it out, and his hand was restored."

The Scriptures say that Jesus was "troubled" and that He "wept" over the death of His close friend, Lazarus (John 11:33-35). At the Mount of Olives, we find Jesus "grieved and distressed" calling upon God to "let this cup pass from Me, yet not as I will, but as Thou wilt" (Matthew 26:36-39).

Jesus, in all of these cases, experienced what we would call negative feelings but did not sin. Why? Because when the feelings came, He made the appropriate response. God never holds us accountable for our feelings, only with what we do with our feelings, our actions.

The first two chapters of this book discussed the many different types of feelings that raising a teenager brings to the surface. To deal with these feelings we must first become aware of them. I first have to become aware that it is *fear* that I feel when I realize that I no longer have absolute control of my teenagers. Once I identify the feeling, I can then deal constructively with it.

The following is a "Feelings Awareness List." Make a check by the feelings that you experience often as a parent of a teenager. Make an "O" by the feelings you rarely experience. Make an exclamation point by the feelings that you experience with great intensity.

Feelings Awareness List

accepted	dependent	impatient
affectionate	disappointed	inadequate
afraid	dominated	incompetent
angry	domineering	in control
anxious	eager to please	inferior
appreciated	embarrassed	inhibited
attractive	envious	insecure
calm	excited	jealous
closed	frustrated	lonely
competent	guilty	lovable
confused	happy	optimistic
creative	hostile	pessimistic
cut off from others	hurt	phony
defeated	ignored	possessive

In addition to becoming aware of my feelings, I need to be able to express these feelings in such a manner that my teenager can hear them. This does not mean that I am entirely responsible for whether my teen actually hears my feelings. It does mean that I am responsible for learning the skill of communicating my feelings accurately.

The Skill of Straight Talk

Start your message with the words "I feel," then *state whatever you feel* in a non-judgmental way. Avoid starting out with "You." Remember it is much easier to talk about the other person. When you start out with "I," it means that you are revealing something personal about yourself. That can be risky, but take the risk. It's worth it. When you say "I feel," you are owning your own feelings. You are simply stating how you feel and not blaming the other person for your feelings.

The second part to "Straight Talk" is to add "when," and then *describe in a non-judgmental way what the situation is.* This is hard to do because we want to attack or blame someone at this point.

The third part of this process is adding the word, "because," and telling why you feel as you do. Let's put it all together now. "I feel *(state whatever you feel)* when *(describe in a non-judgmental way what the situation is)* because *(share what's happening to you because of the situation)."*

Let's take some situations with teenagers and see how this works.

Situation #1: Your teenager has just arrived home from a ball game 45 minutes later than you had agreed upon.
Communication A: "You're late! Why didn't you call? You know you are supposed to call when you're going to be late. I feel like restricting you for a month."
Communication B: "I feel fearful when you are late, because so many things can happen in a car."

Which communication is Straight Talk? Communication B is easier for your teenager to respond to because you are sharing your real feelings. Perhaps your teenager doesn't really understand the anxiety you go through when he is late. When you jump on him the minute he comes in the door (Communication A) he becomes defensive and an ugly scene results. He has done something wrong and that has to be dealt with, but how you communicate your feelings will set the tone for your confrontation. He just might listen and call you the next time he is late, if he really hears how you are feeling.

Let's look at another typical situation.

Situation #2: Your teenager has just left the kitchen a mess for the umpteenth time.

Communication A: "You make me so mad. I try to keep a neat, clean home and you turn it into a pig pen."

Communication B: "I feel resentful and unappreciated when I continually have to pick up after people. Having a clean house is important to me."

In Communication A you have certainly told your teenager how you feel, but not in a way that he will listen. Your teenager will probably become defensive as soon as he hears the word "you" and then get his rebuttal ready. "I clean up most of the time. You don't want people to even live in this house!" The stage is set for a battle royal.

In Communication B you have shared your real feelings in a way that will make it easier for your teenager to respond. You have done a limited amount of blaming and have shared how the situation affects you. In effect, you have said this: "Maybe wanting a spotless house is my problem, but that's the way I am and you could certainly help by being a little more sensitive to my feelings."

You will be amazed at how your teenagers respond when you use this formula.

You can also help your teenagers learn this skill of communication. It will not only help them now, but also for marriage. When Liesl was 15 years old, she once used her skills to express a frustration:

"I feel upset, mad, and very angry when I do one thing wrong and you treat me like a juvenile delinquent, because doing one thing wrong does not make me a juvenile delinquent."

This was accurate communication on Liesl's part. Janet and I needed to hear it. We were not sticking with the issue in our communication with her. We were bringing in too much from the past. It was bogging down our communication.

Straight Talk is a skill that you and your teenagers can learn to use. It does not happen suddenly. This way of communication is one that you have to develop over a long period of time. *It is an ideal to work towards.* Do not expect yourself or your teenagers to use Straight Talk all the time. Our family certainly doesn't. There are times when I choose to revert back to yelling, blaming, and other types of nonproductive communication. However, we do use it *some* of the time and that is an improvement. That skill is always there when we want to call upon it. The more we use it the easier it becomes. Straight Talk takes work to learn and discipline to use, but it is worth the effort!

Four Rules of Parent-Teen Communication

In addition to using Straight Talk, four rules of communication are important for us to learn.

Don't be a faultfinder. As parents of teenagers, Janet and I tend to become faultfinders. In many areas young people do not measure up to our adult standards or meet our expectations. I realize that no human being can become a mature Christian without legitimate criticism in his life. We all have blind spots that hurt our relationship with others. It can be a loving act to share these with one another. However, that criticism must be discerning and discriminate, not angry and hurtful.

God's Word tells us to stop being so critical of one another. "If you must be critical, be critical of yourself and see that you do not cause your brother to stumble" (Romans 14:3).

Faultfinding many times means that we simply will not admit that people are not perfect. Sometimes our faultfinding is a way of hiding our own imperfection by projecting that on others.

Whatever reason for our faultfinding, it is a destructive method of communication. *It just doesn't work.* We may

70

think it works. Our teenagers may comply for a while, but the changes are not permanent. When the pressure is off, it's back to life as usual.

Perhaps the most serious damage it does to a teenager is that it undermines his already shaky self-esteem. Fault-finding makes a teenager feel discouraged. I will never forget the distraught look on Heidi's face a couple of years ago. She had just "finished" her work in the kitchen, and I had jumped on her about something she had not done. She started sobbing and said, "Dad, you and Mom have just been picking me apart. I feel like I can't do anything right anymore." As I followed her down to her room, I began to reflect on the past several weeks. She was right. Janet and I had been on her back continually. Now there were certainly some areas that she needed to shape up, but we had overdone it. We had not balanced criticism with praise. Heidi was feeling like she was worthless. I asked Heidi's forgiveness and started talking to her about the many good qualities she possessed. I shared with her the positive contributions she made to our family. I could immediately see the distressed feeling fade from her eyes. She started relaxing.

"Thanks, Daddy," she said, when I had finished. "That really helps to know that you feel I am special. I was really down on myself."

That day I learned the most important part of criticism—*give praise an equal amount of time.* It is easy to let "maintenance talk" ("Have you done this?" "Why don't you finish this?") dominate our conversation. Communication must include friendly conversation and praise. A second guideline to follow when criticizing your teenagers is, "Criticize the important areas with gentleness and understanding."

Be clear and specific in your communication. One of the biggest pitfalls of parent-teen communication is that of vagueness. Either we are vague ourselves, or we allow our teenagers to be vague in their communication. Either way the results spell disaster.

Let me give you an example. You get up on Saturday morning and have several jobs for family members to do. You ask your son to clean the garage. He says, "Okay, Dad.

I've got some things I have to do first, though. I'll do it a little later."

In your mind, "a little later" means sometime before the day is over. Obviously it meant something else to your son, because three days later he still has not cleaned the garage. You confront your son and he replies, "Dad, I said I would do it a little later and I still will."

There was needless conflict in this situation. The father should have used clear and specific communication. He should have said, "Son, I want you to clean the garage by 5:00 p.m. this afternoon." If the father had not put a specific time limit on the garage, he could have still saved the situation if he had asked his son to be clear and specific. He could have said, "What do you mean by a little later? Exactly what time will you be cleaning the garage?"

Vagueness could have caused further problems in this situation. The father did not define what "clean the garage" meant. His son might have hurriedly swept the floor and thought he was finished (teenagers generally tend to do the least they can get by with). The father sees that there is still junk setting around, and the tools have not been put back in place. He corners his son and says, "I said clean the garage—not rearrange the dirt on the floor." The son replies, "I did what you said, Dad. I cleaned the garage. I didn't know you wanted it hospital clean."

Statements like, "I want you to stop watching so much TV," or, "I want you to improve your grades," are both vague statements that can product conflict. How much do you want your teenager to improve his grades? Exactly how many hours a week do you want your teenager to watch TV? All these questions need to be answered if we are going to be clear and specific in our communication.

Watch out for the expression, "I'll try." "I'll try," is an evasive statement. For example, your daughter has a difficult time getting ready for school and she has missed the school bus several times. You ask her not to miss the school bus anymore. She says, "I'll try." What does that mean? She probably thinks she is already trying. It could be a way to evade making a commitment to getting her act together. The best way of handling this kind of vagueness is to ask, "What do you mean by, 'I'll try?'" Ask her to make specific decisions on how she is going to get ready for school on time. This could include a decision to get her clothes ready the night before or to set her alarm across the room and stay up once she has turned it off.

Clear and specific communication can be a great asset to your relationship to your teenager and the overall atmosphere of your home.

Make realistic statements. Most of us occasionally exaggerate, especially when it comes to the sins of our teenagers. It's not that we have to exaggerate. Our teens goof with sufficient magnitude that we should not have to amplify their sins. However, we do, and it gets us into trouble because they use our exaggerations against us.

For example, you walk into your teenager's room, and it's a disaster. You say, "Why don't you ever clean up your room? It's always a horrible mess." Your teenager jumps right on the opportunity. "What do you mean I never clean my room? I cleaned it last Saturday."

Has this situation ever occurred in your home? You say to your teenager, "You have been on the run constantly for the last two weeks. You haven't spent any time with the family, and you're ruining your health."

Again there is truth in what you have said, but you have exaggerated, and left the door open for the inevitable debate. "Mom, you know that's not true. I was home Wednesday evening."

We must discipline ourselves to make realistic statements. Exaggeration is a poor communication habit that we can break with effort. Making realistic statements removes another conflict hazard from our homes.

Stick to the issue. This is an important rule of communication, especially when conflict is involved. It is also difficult, especially if emotions are strong. Sometimes we don't even know what the issue is. We must define the issue and then stick to it.

Earlier I gave Liesl's Straight Talk statement. She was frustrated because we were not sticking to the issue. We were bringing up her past sins. We really didn't need to do that. The gravity of the one we were talking about was enough. Our energy was being diverted away from solving the problem by being sidetracked by side issues and history.

Teenagers are masters at bringing up many issues when we are having a confrontation with them. Side issues such as, "You're being unfair," or "You don't treat me the same as my brother (sister)," are ways of sidetracking us from the main issue.

Once you have discovered the real issue, try to stick with it. Resist the temptation to bring up past sins. The current problem is enough to deal with. When your teenager's faults are paraded in front of them all at the same time, their self-esteem takes a dive and they angrily defend themselves.

It will help if you can get your teenager to agree with you to stick to the main issue in a confrontation. It is idealistic to think that you will always stick to the issue in conflicts. When you see yourself getting sidetracked, however, take a "time out" and come back to the main issue. The problem will probably not be solved until you do.

Communication is a key to our teenagers. Good communication is an expression of love. Good communication results in intimate relationships build upon trust. It is worth every ounce of effort to expend.

Discussion Questions

1. What one thing causes you the most difficulty when you are trying to communicate with your teenager in a conflict situation?

2. "Feelings are neither good nor bad, but what we do with our feelings is good or bad." What do you think about the author's distinction?

3. Write down the three feelings you most often experience as a parent of a teenager (from the awareness list in this chapter).

4. Write down one Straight Talk statement.

   "I feel _____ when _____

   _____ because _____ ."

5. How do you *feel* about using Straight Talk statements?

6. Make a statement about yourself in regard to fault-finding.

7. Give an example of how the lack of clear and specific communications has caused problems between you and your teenager.

8. Write down one unrealistic statement you have recently made to your teenager.

9. Think about your last confrontation with your teenager. How did sticking or not sticking to the main issue affect your communication?

10. After reading this chapter and evaluating my communication, one thing I will change is ...

CHAPTER 7

Too Big to Spank

I will never forget the scene. My mother and I were living in a small apartment in Los Angeles while my father was on the road holding evangelistic meetings. I can't remember what I did wrong, but my mother was furious. When my mother, a five-foot-tall bundle of energy, became angry she would attack with whatever weapon was within her reach. The weapon closest at hand was a yardstick. As she moved in for the kill, I remember thinking, "No way. She's not going to hit me with that thing. I'm 13 years old and a lot bigger than her." I then used my brute strength to wrestle the weapon away from my mother.

"You can't do this to me," she said in complete frustration. "Wait until your father gets home." I wasn't bothered by the threat because I knew my father wasn't coming home for another three months.

That was my mother's last attempt at physical punishment. She must have realized that it was impractical to try to spank someone bigger and stronger than she was.

There comes a time when our children are too big to spank. Teenagers' physical and emotional maturity make physical discipline inappropriate. It's not just because they are too big, but because of what we are trying to accomplish in their lives.

Janet and I decided that we would no longer spank our children when they entered junior high. We realized that our teens were becoming adults. As parents, the goal of our discipline must be an "inner takeover" by our teenagers. Soon our teens will be free from our restraints and we must trust that they have developed *self-discipline*. Our goal is that by the time they leave home they are well on their way to developing a mature Christian conscience.

Conscience Development

How does that mature Christian conscience develop? Bruce Narramore lists five stages in the development of our children's conscience. Conscience is that part of our personality that evaluates behavior, the inner standards by which we live. If our children are to have Biblical values, they must develop the inner standards of a Christian conscience.

Five Stages of Morality

Morality of physical restraint. During the early months we simply have to restrain our children from dangers. They show almost no sign of a conscience.

Fear and respect. The first signs of conscience begin to appear at the end of the first year and during the second. Your child reaches out to grab a vase off the shelf, and you say "No," emphasized by a swat on his hand. He begins his lessons in fear and respect.

Internalized parent. During this stage children both consciously and unconsciously want to be like their mothers and fathers. This process is known as identification or internalization. They gradually take on our attitudes and values.

The adolescent conscience. During this stage the adolescent begins to reevaluate his standards. He begins to think for himself and no longer takes his parents' attitudes and values as law. The teenager rethinks his morality and comes to his own set of values.

Mature conscience. We should be able to see clear signs of the mature conscience by late adolescence and early adulthood. This means that the conscience should be free from many of the necessary controls of childhood and adolescence. A person with a mature conscience is motivated to Christian behavior because of his love of God and fellow man, not because of external controls and restraints.

We want to launch our teenagers with clear signs of a mature Christian conscience. We want our teens to obey, not because of the fear of punishment, but because their conscience tells them that this is the loving thing to do. We want their concern for others to be shown apart from our watchful eye. *If this inner takeover is going to happen, we must reevaluate our methods of discipline during the teenage years.*

Discipline
First we must reevaluate our definition of discipline. Our attitude towards discipline should be positive. *Discipline* and *disciple* come from the same root word.

> Anyone can punish a child, but only those who can make disciples of the children can truly discipline them. When we see discipline as a positive directive in life, we no longer do something *to* a child, but we do something *for* him or *with* him so that he will want to change for the better. The transfer from the *outward must,* so necessary in infancy, to the *inward ought* as the child grows in understanding, then becomes possible. Each occasion for constructive discipline is only another lesson in a lifelong process of learning, under the guidance of parents and of God.[1]

Punishment is something we do *to* our teenagers. Punishment focuses on the past. Discipline on the other hand is something we do *with* our teenager, focusing on the future.

It is this focus on the future that we observe as we see how God disciplines us. In Hebrews 12:4-13 the spirit and purpose of discipline is given. First we find that when God disciplines us it is a sign of His love. "My son, do not regard lightly the discipline of the Lord, Nor faint when you are reproved by Him; For those whom the Lord loves He disciplines, and He scourges every son whom He receives" (Hebrews 12:5, 6). We discipline our teenagers because we love them and they realize they are loved because of our discipline.

A second purpose of discipline is to help build holiness in our children. This is God's purpose of discipline in our lives. "For they disciplined us for a short time as seemed best to them, but He disciplines us for our good that we may share in His holiness. All discipline for the moment seems not to be joyful, but sorrowful; yet to those who have been trained by it, afterwards it yields the peaceful fruit of righteousness" (Hebrews 12:10, 11).

As Christian parents, we are compelled to discipline our teenagers. Their very holiness is at stake. We all try to avoid pain in our lives. Our teenagers will try to avoid the pain of discipline. As parents we will try to avoid the paid of administering discipline. But we must remember that the purpose of discipline is to show love and produce a harvest of righteousness and peace in our children.

Methods of Discipline

The question still remains, "What do I do when they're too big to spank?" Our children still need discipline. They disobey. We draw a line and they put their foot over that line. We see our teens as insensitive, immature at many levels, and irresponsible. These attitudes and actions call for some kind of discipline.

Expectations

Before looking at methods of discipline, we first need to examine our expectations for our teenagers. Many problems surface because we either do not have clear-cut expectations for our teenagers, or we have not communicated our expectations. Either way we can expect frustrations. Exactly what are your expectations for your teenager in regard to dating? When can your teenager start dating? What age person can he or she date? What will the curfew be? What are your standards on dating a Christian or non-Christian? Where do you draw the line on physical contact? How about school? What grades and attitudes do you expect? What about chores around the house? What do you expect in the way of friends, car, family time, activities, church, curfew, finances, work?

If we do not have clear-cut expectations for our teenagers, and communicate these expectations, we find ourselves in a position of continually reacting. For example, you have not had clear communication on when your teenager is to date. She is asked out on a date, tells the boy yes, and then asks for your permission. Because you didn't act earlier you find yourself reacting. You have a confrontation and your teenager says, "why didn't you tell me I couldn't date?" You answer, "why didn't you ask first?" The whole scene could have been avoided by a thorough discussion of dating standards at an earlier date.

Sit down with your spouse and make a list of your expectations. Talk to your teenager about these expectations. Ask him about *his* expectations. Be open to negotiations in some of these areas. If your teenager sees these expectations as another Ten Commandments set in stone, then there will be a little communication. Respect his thoughts. Remember you are looking for the "inner takeover."

Communication

I am convinced that communication is the best method of discipline we can use. By talking to our teenagers we show them respect. They feel that we are respecting their ability to reason and their desire to make changes in their own lives. Communication as a method of discipline helps our teens *evaluate their behavior,* especially if we communicate effectively.

Janet and I found that it is *our* attitude that sets the pace for using communication as a method of discipline (or any other method, for that matter). When we start out talks with our teenagers with prayer, the entire conversation takes on a new dimension. We are inviting God to be a part of the discipline process. It is extremely difficult to ask God's help and then ignore the attitudes that God expects from us. Every discussion we have started with prayer has softened our attitude and the attitude of our teenagers. The result has been increased understanding from loving communication. On the other hand, when we have gone into a confrontation with the wrong attitudes, the discussions have deteriorated to fights. *As parents we set the pace.* Our teens will many times follow our example.

The goals of communication as a method of discipline is to help our teens form a godly conscience from which to make decisions.

Natural Consequences

God has a way of disciplining us with natural consequences. If I eat too much, then I get a stomachache. If I am not a good steward of my money, then I have to pay the consequences with overdue bills, failure to provide for my family, and a host of other painful experiences. God does not bail me out. He allows me to experience the natural consequences of my actions so I can learn correct behavior. If God paid off my bills whenever I have not been using money wisely, He would be contributing to my immaturity. God, being the perfect Father, does not do that. I know that my heavenly Father hates to see me suffer, but He knows that the result will be maturity and happiness in my life.

One of our teenage daughters thought that money was something you got rid of as fast as possible. She evidently believed that she would contact some kind of terminal disease if she was in possession of money for too long a time. One summer we planned to vacation in Southern California with another family. The girls had been looking forward to this vacation for over a year. They diligently saved their money for this trip, except Liesl. Liesl had other things to spend her money on—presents for friends, clothes, and basketball camp. Two weeks before our vacation it hit her. She was almost broke. She pleaded with us for extra work. She scrimped and saved, but it was too late. We refused to bail her out. We allowed God to teach her a lesson through natural consequences.

Logical Consequences

Logical consequences differ from natural consequences because we are involved in structuring the consequence of misbehavior. When our teenager has misbehaved, we find a consequence that is closely associated with the action.

Here are some examples of logical consequences. Your son has been using the family car. You have communicated to him your expectation that he drive no faster than the speed limit. Word gets back to you that he is trying to see how fast the car would go on a "safe" stretch of road. The logical consequence of your son's actions could be that he lose the privilege of driving the car for one month.

Your daughter comes home from a date an hour late and did not call you. After some communication, you realize that the time just "got away" because she was having a good conversation with her boy friend. A logical consequence could be that she must "pay back" the hour with interest that hour by being home two hours earlier on the next date.

Your teenager refuses to clean up his room. Nothing seems to work. You could clean up your teenager's room and charge him normal maid service wages.

Logical consequences is one of the best methods of discipline to use with teenagers. You show your teen that he is responsible for his actions. When he chooses to misbehave he will then suffer logical consequences for those actions.

Three Difficult Tasks of Parenting

Managing Anger

Part of living with a teenager means dealing with anger, yours and his. An adolescent experiences many angry feelings as a natural part of his move toward discovery of self and independence. Sometimes we take the brunt of those angry feelings. How we deal with our own angry feelings is a critical part of positive parent-teen relations.

You have asked your teenager to do some simple chores around the house. Two days later those chores remain untouched. The result—anger. We may deny that it is anger. We will probably call our feelings frustration, irritation, or some other word to camouflage our anger, but the fact remains, we are angry. Why? Because we have had an expectation that has not been met. Unmet expectations are the source of much of our anger.

Your teenager asks you if he can stay overnight with a friend. He has homework to do and has had a hectic week. You deny the request. Your teenager becomes angry and goes into a tirade about your unfairness. You have just become the focus of an attack that you did not deserve. The result—anger.

In the last chapter we discussed Jesus' anger with the Pharisees. He was angry about the sin in their lives and confronted it. The anger Jesus showed was not sinful because it was righteous anger. It was properly directed. "There are several characteristics of righteous anger: First of all it must be managed, not heated, nor unrestrained passion. Second, there must be no hatred, malice, or resentment. A third characteristic of righteous anger is that its motivation is unselfish. Another characteristic of righteous anger is that it is directed against wrong deeds or situations, not against people."[2]

On the other hand *unrighteous* anger can hurt our relationship with our teenagers. "Let every one be quick to hear, slow to speak and slow to anger; for the anger of man does not achieve the righteousness of God" (James 1:19, 20).

The "anger of man" is not righteous anger. It is not managed anger and will not solve problems or build positive relationships with your teenagers.

Unmanaged anger hinders our communication. First, our teenager becomes defensive. We cannot think as clearly when we are angry. It interferes with our entire communication process.

It is possible to become angry and not sin. Paul himself said, "Be angry, and yet do not sin" (Ephesians 4:26). The challenge we have as parents of teenagers is to be aware of our anger and manage it. Denying our anger will only cause severe problems.

Anger is energy. You could look at it as a ball of fire in your stomach. That energy has to have some outlet. If you let that ball of fire remain in your stomach, destructive things will happen. Your anger might leak out a little at a time, slicing at your teenager with cutting remarks, faultfinding or non-verbal actions. Your anger might build up until it explodes, causing serious damage. There is also the possibility that your "ball of fire" will turn on you and cause depression, ulcers, or other physical or mental problems.

God does not want us to deal with our anger in counterproductive ways. Here are some constructive ways of dealing with your anger.

—Recognize that you are angry. Don't deny your anger. Become aware of your feelings.

—Ask yourself, "Where is my anger coming from? Is it unmet expectations? Does my anger come from my own feelings of inadequacy?"

—Understand why you are angry. Is it because you cannot stand your teenager being angry with you? Do you feel unloved when someone is directing their anger towards you? Do you feel helpless in the situation?

—Ask yourself, "How can I deal with my anger?" Sometimes you will need to confront your teenager. Many times it is best to go directly to the source of the anger. If you do, remember to use your Straight Talk skills. ("I *feel* angry *when* I have worked hard cleaning the house and you make a mess, *because* I feel unappreciated.") There are times when you can deal with your anger by talking to another person-preferably the parent of another teenager. They understand!

Another way of handling anger constructively is to channel it. I work off a lot of anger by jogging and playing racquetball. I have a friend that works off his by chopping wood. *The best way of handling anger is going to the source*—your teenager. This can resolve the feelings permanently and promote understanding.

We can manage our angry feelings much better when we realize that our teenager's overreaction is helping him release his stored up anger and frustrations, but we are a handy dumping ground for our teenagers. Where else can he get away with such atrocities? Understanding this can help us not to take his anger personally. Managing our anger and handling our teenager's anger is one of the most difficult tasks we face as parents.

Showing Forgiveness

It's not easy to be on the giving end of forgiveness most of the time, but as parents of teenagers, that is where we consistently find ourselves. Sometimes we would like to have our teenagers *ask* us for forgiveness. That will come with time. Meanwhile, no matter how difficult it seems, we must model the godly quality of forgiveness for our teenagers. Where else will they learn?

We are told to "forgive as the Lord forgave you" (Colossians 3:13), and "Be kind to one another, tender-hearted, forgiving each other, just as God in Christ also has forgiven you" (Ephesians 4:32).

Forgiving teenagers is difficult. Our teenager has "burned" us for the fifth straight time. Direct disobedience each time. Are we still to forgive? *How is this possible?*

Christ's example makes forgiving our teenagers possible. We need to remember how God continually forgives us, *often for the same offense.* How many times will God forgive us? As many times as we need forgiveness!

Our forgiveness by God comes at a great personal price to Him. God paid an immeasurable cost for our forgiveness. Christ suffered and died as a penalty for our sin (1 Peter 2:21-25). *God paid a debt for us that He did not owe.* He simply offered us the gift of forgiveness.

Forgiveness of our teenagers many times comes at a great personal price to us also. We have been betrayed. We are hurt and disappointed. We offer our forgiveness as a gift, not because our teenager deserves it. This is the way God comes to us. He simply forgives us because of His great love for us. It is a decision God has made.

Because of our great love for our teenagers we forgive them. Because of what God has done for us we will forgive them seventy times seven times. We will forgive them regardless of our feelings at the time because we have *decided* to forgive as God has forgiven us.

We can learn great lessons about forgiveness from living with teenagers. Janet and I learned such a lesson. One of our daughters have just grieved us by flagrantly disobeying a hard and fast rule. What was more infuriating, she wouldn't even admit to the fact that she had disobeyed, even though there were ample witnesses.

Our response as parents was totally wrong. We broke all the principles I just mentioned about managing anger. Our daughter showed us that she was capable of just as much unmanaged anger as we were.

You could slice the tension in our house with a knife for the next several days. This was unusual, because we generally are able to resolve issues when they arise. Things got worse instead of better, in spite of a couple of feeble attempts by myself to ask forgiveness for my anger. The issue of the disobedience was still unresolved.

Janet and I came to a place where we realized that outside counsel was needed to help sort out our feelings and actions. We called up some good friends with godly wisdom and asked to see them. We explained our feelings and the situation of this couple. I was not prepared for their counsel.

"Sometimes we simply decide to forgive our teenagers without completely resolving the situation," they said. "We have gone to our teenager and said, 'Let's wipe the slate clean and start all over. We forgive you, and the matter will not be discussed again.'"

As I listened to this counsel, I began to have a peace about the situation. I realized that this was what Janet and I had to do. Our attitudes had been wrong and we had found out why the Scriptures say, "The anger of man does not achieve the righteousness of God" (James 1:20).

Janet and I called our daughter into our room. Her body language said, loud and clear, *"Now* what?"

I said, "Honey, your mother and I have decided that we want to wipe the slate clean on this situation and start all over. Our attitudes were not right. What you did was wrong, but we want to forgive you and not mention the incident again."

Our daughter looked at us very suspiciously. Her eyes said, "What's going on here? What's the catch?" She said. "I don't understand." So we explained our decision again.

As our daughter began to feel the effects of the forgiveness that was given to her, we could visibly see her begin to relax and soften. The pent up hostility began to melt away. It really was a new start. Janet and I learned the valuable lesson that sometimes you simply have to forgive and start over regardless of the situation. Isn't that what God does with us?

Demonstrating Trust

We have forgiven our teenager. It's not the first time, and we are beginning to wonder whether we should trust him. He picks up our lack of trust and says, "You don't trust me."

You answer, "How can I trust you when you continue to abuse your car privileges? I ask you to drive with no more than four people in the car and I find that you have packed six kids into that Toyota again. You are going to have to *earn* my trust."

Is this fair? Is it possible? Does God ask us to "earn" His trust when we have sinned? No. He trusts us once again to do His will. Like forgiveness, His trust is a gift.

How could the incident with the car be handled? Certainly there must be some discipline.

I could say, "Son, you want us to trust you to use your best judgment. Okay, we will. We want you to trust us to use our best judgment in setting a few limits . . ."

It's possible to affirm trust in your son when rejecting untrustworthy acts. "Saying, 'I'll trust you to try again—in a better way,' opens the door to understanding. Trust is love that forgets the past, reaches out here and now to believe and encourages others, and gives them the freedom to claim the future."[3]

I agree that this kind of trust is difficult. Our human reaction is to make our teenagers earn our trust. There are consequences for breaking trust. We always must ask for responsible action. We must also *trust again,* as God trusts us.

What do we do when they're too big to spank? We love them. We discipline them with a goal of right living. We forgive them and trust them as God forgives and trusts us. This is quite a challenge. Remember, *what God expects, God enables.*

---

[1]Bruce Narramore, *An Ounce of Prevention.* Grand Rapids, MI: Zondervan 1973, pp. 67-85.

²H. Norman Wright, *The Christian Use of Emotional Power.* Old Tappan, NJ: Revell, 1974, pp. 113-115.

³David Augsburger, *Caring Enough to Confront.* Ventura, CA: Regal, 1980, p. 67.

Discussion Questions

1. Complete the following sentences:
   "What I do when they're too big to spank is _____

   _____."

   "My biggest frustration when they're too big to spank is

   _____."

2. Read Hebrews 12:4-13 and then write your definition of discipline.

3. What method of discipline do you use most with your teenagers?

4. What signs do you see that your teenager is developing a mature conscience?

5. Think of a time when communication as a method of discipline has worked well for you.

6. Think of a logical consequence you could use to help your teenager overcome a behavior that irritates you.

7. The author gives insights on managing anger. Rate yourself on a scale of 1-10, first on your ability to manage your own anger, and second, to handle the anger of your teenager.

8. Finish the sentence, "Showing forgiveness to my teenager is

   _____."

9. What are some of the ideas you struggled with as you read the author's comments on trust?

10. After reading this chapter and evaluating myself, one thing I will change to improve the discipline of my teenager is ...

CHAPTER 8

Hormones, Dating, and Love

You feel the palms of your hands start to moisten. Beads of perspiration are starting to pop out on your forehead. Your heart rate has increased to at least 140 beats per minute. You look for someplace to hide, but there is no way of escape. Your 14-year-old daughter has just announced that she has been asked on a date alone and has accepted. Now you must answer. Thoughts race through your mind at the speed of sound. Is he a Christian? What if he uses drugs or alcohol? What kind of family does he come from?

"We haven't even discussed dating," you protest. "You're too young to be going on a date alone. You should know that."

Perhaps your daughter has gone about things the wrong way, but the fact is that you failed to prepare yourself and your teenager for the inevitable question of dating.

Preparing our teenagers for dating is one of the most important tasks we have as parents. It is also one of the most difficult and most threatening. We have our own past to deal with. Our dating experiences—insecurities, rejections, physical involvement—all influence the way we handle dating with our teenagers.

The best way to prepare our sons and daughters for dating is to face the issues openly. I suggest that every family develop a Dating Covenant early in teenage years. This covenant needs not only your input, but also the thoughts and feelings of your teenagers. A Dating Covenant is something that you work out together. It should be mutually acceptable to both you and your teenagers.

I recommend two books that you and your teenagers should read. These books are *Givers, Takers, and Other Kinds of Lovers* by Josh McDowell and *Update* by Fred Hartley.

Dating Covenant

Following is list of thirteen questions for you to ask yourself. Write the answers down on a piece of paper. Husbands and wives should work on these questions together. Then copy the questions and have your teenagers answer them on paper. Next, discuss your answers. The goal of this time is to communicate with one another on feelings and expectations about dating. You need to know how your teenager feels and your teenager needs your input. The final outcome of these sessions should be a mutually acceptable Dating Covenant.

At the end of each set of questions I include Janet's and my conclusions on the questions. There is no way I can answer these questions *for you*. You have your own Christian life to draw on; you will have your own way of looking at some of these questions. The discussion after each question is to stimulate your thinking and help you and your teen arrive at *your dating standards.*

Questions for You to Answer

1. *What is the purpose of dating?* Seldom do teenagers really think of the purpose of dating. It is just something that seems natural to do. Understanding the purpose of dating will help your teenagers develop a more mature dating policy.

Dates are the building blocks to marriage. Josh McDowell and Paul Lewis in their excellent book, *Givers, Takers, and Other Kinds of Lovers*, share this purpose. "One of the first purposes is socialization. As we mature, our skills in interpersonal relationships, conversation and understanding need to grow up with us. Dating is terrific way to learn more about yourself, to become skilled at sensing the needs and feelings of another person, and to learn how to turn that insight into responsive action. Good dating prepares you for a happy, growing and lasting marriage."[1]

A second purpose of dating is to find out what kind of a mate is desired for marriage. Through dating, a teenager is exposed to a variety of character traits. They will find themselves being attracted to some of these character traits. They will find themselves being attracted to some of these character traits and repelled by others. Dating a variety of different people helps your teenager recognize the type of person he wants to marry.

It is easy for teenagers to date for all the wrong reasons—sexual attraction, social status, etc. It is our duty as parents to help our teenagers think through proper motivations for dating.

2. *When should my teen start dating?* Janet and I feel that placing an exact age on dating can be a disadvantage. For example, your first child might be a very responsible teenager (this is the way it is many times with firstborn children). You decide that 15 is an appropriate age to date and you inform your oldest child. Your second child, of course, hears this and assumes that 15 is the age he can date. What happens if your next child does not show the maturity and responsibility to date when he is 15? Do you see the problem? One teenager might be mature enough to date alone at 15, while the other is barely mature enough at 17.

The privilege to date should be tied to other types of responsible action by your teenagers. This can be communicated early in the teenage years. For example, dating might be tied to being home from activities on time, noticeable spiritual growth, trustworthiness in the freedoms they already have, good judgment in friends, and so on. If your teenager knows these are your expectations, they can become goals for him to work toward.

It is, however, good to have in your mind some general

age guidelines as to when the "average" teenager could start dating.

3. *Should my teen date non-Christians?* Let's think back to the two purposes of dating mentioned earlier. One of the purposes is the future selection of a mate. *At some time one of your teenager's dates will lead to marriage.* What if the date is with a non-Christian? I know of many Christian young people who have been trapped by "missionary dating." The convert in the final result was himself, not the person they were trying to lead to the Lord. Often dating a non-Christian results in the spiritual deterioration of the Christian. When the dating of a non-Christian results in marriage, there is often pain and division in the home.

What does God's Word have to say about Christians dating non-Christians? Nothing. The Bible does not mention dating, but it does give standards for marriage. The Scriptures also give guidelines for friendships.

In the Old Testament God instructed the Israelites not to marry foreign wives (Deuteronomy 7:3). The Jews did not pay attention to God's wishes and paid the consequences time after time (Ezra 10).

In the New Testament it is assumed that Christians will marry Christians. 1 Corinthians 7:39 says, "A wife is bound as long as her husband lives; but if her husband is dead, she is free to be married to whom she wishes, only in the Lord."

Another New Testament passage applies here. "Do not be bound together with unbelievers; for what partnership have righteousness and lawlessness, or what fellowship has light with darkness? Or what harmony has Christ with Belial, or what has a believer in common with an unbeliever?" (2 Corinthians 6:14, 15)

Now this Scripture is not dealing directly with marriage or dating, but the principle, "What has a believer in common with an unbeliever?" fits. If the most important single thing in your life is a vital relationship with Christ, what common ground is there for dating? It seems to me that a huge element of the relationship is being neglected. Dating can easily lead to being "bound together," in an emotional attachment. Once this emotional bonding happens it is extremely difficult for a Christian to get out of the relationship.

In my opinion it is best for our teens to date only Christians. With my girls, that did not always happen (in some cases, to their detriment). It is also my opinion, after much struggling in this area, that the ultimate decision should be made by our teenagers. We have a responsibility to discuss our convictions with them. They have a responsibility to God to do what they think is right.

4. *What are appropriate activities to do on a date?* Dating should provide a climate in which two people can become good friends. Activities for dates should be chosen that will move teenagers toward that goal. Activities such as sporting events, visits to a zoo or historical points of interest, parties, Christian fellowships, beach outings, tennis, and plays or musicals, can help teens become good friends.

We need to casually suggest various types of activities for our teens to do on dates. Many times they don't know what to do, and they will take our advice after initially acting like each thing we mention is 20 years out of date.

5. *What is the curfew for dates?* This will depend largely on the type of activity that your teens are doing. Rather than a particular time, Janet and I would rather discuss each activity separately. It is my feeling that teenagers ought to have specific plans and an adequate estimate of how much time they will need for an activity. I believe it is unwise to allow our teens to "go somewhere and find something to do." Too much unstructured time together brings up the temptation of physical involvement.

Giving our teens an adequate amount of time for their activity, and time to have dessert afterwards, is appropriate. It is also reasonable to ask them to come into the house when they arrive home. If they want to spend some more time together, allow them the privacy to do that in your house. This is far superior to spending an excessive amount of time in the car. Make sure that they know they are *welcome* in your home, and that they can have some space of their own.

6. *How often can my teen date each week?* This, of course, will be open to negotiation with your teenager, but it is good to have a general rule in mind. In my estimation, one formal date a week is plenty. There may be church activities or other activities that do not constitute an actual date. Our teens usually have busy schedules, and keeping dating to once a week will help them discipline themselves to accomplish other important things in their lives.

7. *How physically involved should my teen become with a boyfriend or girlfriend?* First, we need to recognize that many teenagers are sexually active today. An article on teenage sex in *Newsweek* revealed the following: "The latest figures in a highly respected new study by Johns Hopkins University professors Melvin Zelnik and John F. Kantner indicates that nearly 50% of the nation's 10.3 million young women, age 15-19, have had premarital sex. The percentage has nearly doubled since Zelnik and Kantner began their surveys in 1971."[2]

Society's moral standards are putting pressure on ourselves and our teens. As parents our responsibility is to help our teens maintain high standards in their sexuality, and at the same time understand the normal pressures of adolescence and the pressures of the peer group. Your daughter needs to know that boys are more sexually aggressive than girls. Girls are often satisfied with kissing and being close and are unaware of the intense desire that love play arouses in boys. Boys, on the other hand, need to discipline themselves not to put pressure for physical contact on girls.

Our teenagers need to understand what Josh McDowell and Paul Lewis call the "Law of Diminishing Returns." "One kind of physical contact satisfies for awhile, and then it starts to wear off. Then you have to have a little more and that starts to wear off. Then a little more and a little more. You go a little further and a little further still, and before you know it, you've gone too far."[3]

The time for your teenagers to decide where they will set the limit for physical contact is *before they start dating.* They need to remind themselves of the purposes for dating. Dating is for socialization and mate selections, not to prepare for sexual intercourse. Sexual foreplay is for the purpose of preparing for intercourse, a totally different purpose than dating.

It is understandable that your teens will have physical contact with their dates. While developing a dating policy, it is a good time to discuss what the limitations will be.

Most of us are unaware of where our teenagers stand on the issue of physical involvement in dating. What's more we find it a difficult issue on which to become specific. H. Norman Wright, in his helpful booklet, *An Answer to Parent-Teen Relationships*, gives a chart of sexual behavior that you can use with your teens.

The examples on the chart indicate the various ways people express their affection to one another. The styles of sexual expression for four different couples has been indicated. The first couple engages in all the various sexual activities very rapidly. The second couple leaves only sexual inter-

Sexual Behavior

L = Look
T = Touch
h = Holding hands
      lightly
H = Holding hands
      constantly
k = Light kiss

K = Strong kiss
K = French kiss
B = Fondling of
      breasts
SO = Sexual organs
SI = Sexual intercourse

LT	hHkKKB	SO SI		
LT	h H k	K **K**	B SO	SI
LT	h H	k K	**K**	B SO SI
LT	h H	k	K	**K** B SO SI
Friendship	Dating	Going Steady	Engagement	Marriage

Figure 8-1. Sexual Behavior

course for marriage. They have done everything else and these individuals are sometimes referred to as technical virgins. The third couple has gone as far as french kissing prior to marriage, and left everything else for marriage. The chart is explained by the parents to their teens who are then asked to draw what they feel their own standard should be in their dating life. Reasons for the standard should be given and discussed openly.[4]

This can be a tool in deciding with your teen what the limits of physical contact will be.

To better understand the current sexual pressures teenagers face, I suggest reading Josh McDowell and Dick Day's book, *Why Wait? What You Need to Know About the Teen Sexuality Crisis.*

8. *Do I expect my son or daughter to introduce me to dates prior to the time of the date?* I would like this to happen, but it is not a hard and fast rule in our dating policy. So far, our girls have dated mostly boys that we know from our church. Another alternative is for the boy to come early and visit for a few minutes or for the boy to take the girl to meet his parents before the date.

9. *What qualities should my teen look for in the person he or she dates?* It is good to discuss your feelings about desirable character qualities. Perhaps your teen has never really sat down and thought out the kind of person he/she would like to someday marry. This is a good discipline that can help your teens start the refining process that is essential to finding a life partner. It is not that they are to look for the "perfect person," but that they have in mind godly qualities they expect in the person they someday want to marry. While the age of the person your teen is going to date is not a quality, it is an issue. It is my feeling that it is unwise to date someone who is three or more years older.

10. *What qualities does my teen possess that will make him/her a desirable date?* Think through the character qualities that will someday make your teen a good marriage partner. Is your teen sensitive to the feelings of others? Does your teen have a servant's heart? Does he control his anger? Does your teen show self-discipline?

97

It will be interesting to compare your list of positive qualities to the list your teenager has made about himself. In your discussion it will be important to praise his positive qualities, but also helpful if you will point out some blind spots. Help your teenager to set some goals to build godly character qualities in his life.

11. *How should my teenager accept a date, turn down a date, and terminate a dating relationship?* Our teenagers would like us to think they know more about dating than they really do. Many times they are greatly lacking in some basic skills of dating. Boys, for example, need to know how to ask for a date. I can remember being so afraid of rejection when I was a teenager that I left myself every way of escape. I would ask questions like, "What are you doing Friday night?" Or have a friend check out the girl to see if she would go out with me, if I asked.

"Our son needs to know that a 'no' from a girl does not mean that she has rejected him. There can be many reasons for the 'no' and she does not owe him an explanation. A simple question from the boy can help a girl formulate her answer. 'I'm going to the show tonight, will you go with me?' would be appropriate.

"Our daughters can use some help as well. An answer like, 'Thank you, but I have other plans,' is easier for him than a flat no. It is also better than an excuse like, 'I've got to stay home and study.'"[5] If she really likes the boy and would like to go out with him some other time, she could say, "Why don't you ask again sometime?"

You should teach your sons to always come to the door and talk to the girl's folks. I always appreciate it when the *boy* tells me of his plans for the evening, without me asking. I don't like to look like I'm prying, but I need to hear *from him* as well as my daughter where they are going and what time they will be back.

Your daughter needs to know how to end a date. It is preferable that she invite the boy in for a few minutes than to sit in front of the house in a car.

Our teenagers should know how to terminate a dating relationship—that is, a steady dating situation. The immature way is to have a friend break the news. The cruel way is to start acting distant or hostile to the individual. There is always the phone, but that too can be an easy way out. The mature way to end a dating relationship is a gentle face-to-face encounter, being as honest as possible without being cruel.

I recently witnessed one of our daughters go through the agony of breaking up with a boy. She was tempted by all the easy ways out, but finally decided (with a little prodding from her father) to talk face-to-face. She actually wrote out what she wanted to say. I read her notes and suggested a couple of changes. The encounter went much better than she expected, and she and the boy are still good friends.

12. *What is the difference between romantic love and marriage love?* Society at large, and the media in particular, present such a distorted definition of love that it is no wonder our teenagers are confused. Love is either presented as lust or a temporary feeling. When the feeling is gone, then love is no longer there. Our world presents a self-seeking kind of love. Even Christians are confused about real love. When a Christian couple comes to me for counseling, far too often one will say, "I don't love him/her anymore." I'll ask how they came to that conclusion and they will say, "Because I don't have any *feelings* for him/her anymore."

Since when is Christian love just a feeling? The Bible defines love as a decision, a commitment. The Bible rarely speaks of feelings of love, but consistently talks about acts of love (1 Corinthians 13).

The apostle John defines real love:

> Beloved, let us love one another, for love is from God; and every one who loves is born of God and knows God. The one who does not love does not know God, for God is love. By this the love of God was manifested in us, that God has sent His only begotten Son into the world so that we might live through Him. In this is love, not that we loved God, but that He loved us and sent His Son to be the propitiation for our sins. Beloved, if God so loved us, we ought to love one another (1 John 4:7-11).

Biblical love is a decision. It is a commitment. It is not "love if" or "love because." It is unconditional with no strings attached. God simply decided to give His love to us. He does not withdraw His love when we disappoint Him.

Obviously, this is also the definition of *marriage love.* We make a decision to love someone and that is a commitment for life. It is not based upon the unpredictable whims of our temporary feelings. *Marriage love* carries with it the decision to love one person in a special way—to become one with that person in a lifelong commitment of marriage.

Romantic love, on the other hand, is largely dependent upon feelings. Romantic love is a necessary step for your teenager to take to prepare him for marriage love. As adults we know that romantic teenage love is not enduring, is full of jealousies, misunderstandings, and self-centeredness. Our teenagers, however, must invest strong love feelings in others to move toward a mature marriage love. *But they need to accept romantic love for what it is.* It is not marriage love!

The problem comes in trying to convince our teenagers that the romantic feelings they have are not forever. The delicate balance comes from teaching what real love is and understanding and respecting the intensity of their teenage romantic love. Labeling it as "puppy love" or making light of their romantic love is not the answer. It is real to them at the moment. We need to warn our teenagers about saying "I love you" to a girlfriend or boyfriend. Do they mean romantic love or do they mean marriage love? How does the other person interpret, "I love you"?

I feel it is essential that your teenagers know the difference between marriage love and romantic love. Part of your dating covenant should be a mutually acceptable definition of love. Reading *Givers, Takers, and Other Kinds of Lovers* and *Update* in addition to Scriptures on love will provide the resources for this definition. Dr. James Dobson also gives a helpful test on love in his book and tapes, *Preparing for Adolescence.*

13. *How soon should my teenager make a permanent commitment to his or her girlfriend or boyfriend (promise to marry)?* Too many teenagers make the mistake of promising to marry at too early an age. Teenagers can be intensely loyal. Because they have made such a commitment

they will hold to it tenaciously even when all counsel is opposed. This seems to be especially true among strong-willed children.

I personally feel that few high school young people are ready to choose a mate and make a decision of *marriage love.* This takes mature experience and reasoning that only comes with age. The tremendous divorce rate among teenage marriages bears this out. I feel we need to ask our teenagers not to make a commitment to marriage at least until they have graduated from high school.

One final thought on love and marriage. Every day we are preparing our teenagers for love and marriage. It is our example that will have the greatest impact on their attitudes and expectations. If they see that we have unconditional love for our spouse, if we live out godly love in our home, then our teenagers will learn God's greatest lesson firsthand.

Questions for Your Teenagers to Answer

Make a list of the following questions and ask your teenager to write out the answers. Explain that you are doing the same questions and that you will have some sessions to work on a dating covenant.

1. What is the purpose of dating?

2. When should I start dating?

3. Should I date non-Christians?

4. What are appropriate activities to do on a date?

5. What is the curfew for dates?

6. How often should I be allowed to date each week?

7. How physically involved should I become with a boyfriend or girlfriend?

8. Should I introduce my date to my parents before the first date occurs?

9. What qualities should I look for in the person I date?

10. What qualities do I possess that will make me a desirable date?

11. How should I accept a date, turn down a date, and terminate a dating relationship?

12. What is the difference between romantic love and marriage love?

13. How soon should I make a permanent commitment (a promise to marry) to a girlfriend or boyfriend?

Conclusion

It will probably take several sessions to discuss all these areas and develop a mutually acceptable dating covenant. When the covenant has been developed, make copies for yourself and your teenager. The time you spend on this project will help build a positive relationship with your teens.

Developing a covenant, however, is no assurance that your teenager will always abide by the covenant. A covenant is only as good as the word of the parties making the covenant. In the case of maturing teenagers, they sometimes change their minds. If the covenant was developed at age 14, at age 16 they have different thoughts. It might be good to renegotiate the covenant each year.

---

[1] Josh McDowell and Paul Lewis, *Givers, Takers, and Other Kinds of Lovers.* Wheaton, IL: Tyndale, 1980, pp. 94, 95.

[2] "Games Teenagers Play," *Newsweek*, September 1, 1980, p. 48.

[3] McDowell and Lewis, p. 86.

[4] Norman Wright, *An Answer to Parent-Teen Relationships.* Eugene, OR: Harvest House, 1977, pp. 47, 48.

[5] Jay Kesler, *Too Big to Spank.* Ventura, CA: Regal, 1978, p. 72.

Discussion Questions

1. Think back to your teenage years. Were your dating experiences negative or positive? How did you feel about your parents dating policies for you?

2. Give some of your thoughts about the purpose of dating.

3. What do you feel is an appropriate age for teens to start dating?

4. Do you think your teens should date non-Christians? Why or why not?

5. How often and how late should teens be allowed to date?

6. The author quotes Josh McDowell's concept of the "Law of Diminishing Returns." How do you think this concept affects the spiritual life of a teenager?

7. Is it reasonable to expect your son or daughter to introduce you to dates prior to the date?

8. What indications have you seen that your teen does or does not understand the difference between romantic love and marriage love?

9. How do you feel about developing a "dating covenant" with your teenager?

10. After reading this chapter, one thing I will do to improve this area of communication with my teenager is . . .

CHAPTER 9

Three Great Life Goals for Teenagers

Unless the Lord builds the house,
They labor in vain who build it;
Unless the Lord guards the city,
The watchman keeps awake in vain.
It is vain for you to rise up early,
To retire late,
To eat the bread of painful labors;
For He gives to His beloved even in his sleep.

Behold, children are a gift of the Lord;
The fruit of the womb is a reward,
Like arrows in the hand of a warrior,
So are the children of one's youth.
How blessed is the man whose quiver is full of them;
They shall not be ashamed,
When they speak with their enemies in the gate.

Psalm 127

There are several great truths in this beautiful passage on the family. First *the Lord builds our families.* God is the master builder, and we are His laborers. We work from His blueprint and under His authority. Secondly, *our children are a gift.* While in today's society our children are no longer economic assets as they were in Biblical days, they still remain our most precious possessions. Thirdly, *our children are like arrows.* Any of you that have shot a bow knows that you aim the arrows carefully at a target. This is the function of a bow and arrow. The purpose God has given us for our children is to *aim them at three great life goals.*

Three Great Life Goals

The three great life goals God wants us to aim our children toward are these: a vital relationship with God, a vital relationship with others, and a vital relationship with themselves.

How do we know that these are the goals that God wants us to set for our teenagers? Jesus gave these three vital goals of life when a lawyer asked Him the question, "'Teacher, which is the great commandment in the Law?' and He said to him, 'You shall love the Lord your God with all your heart, and with all your soul, and with all your mind.' This is the great and foremost commandment. And a second is like it, 'You shall love your neighbor as yourself.' On these two commandments depend the whole Law and the Prophets" (Matthew 22:36-40).

Jesus is saying that there are three vital areas in our life: our love for God, our love for others and our love for ourselves (implied). This last vital relationship may be controversial to some. I am not saying here that we should have a self-centered love for ourselves. I do believe we are to look at ourselves as God looks at us—as His beloved children purchased with the blood of Christ. We know that God does not want us to have an inflated view of ourselves, but neither do I believe He wants us to have a deflated view of ourselves. People I have counseled with who have the lowest self-esteem also have the most difficulty loving others and understanding God's love for themselves.

The development of these three vital life relationships are your teenager's life goals. How well your teenager learns these relationships will determine the quality of his Christian life and his success as an individual.

Ideally, we have been aiming our teenagers toward these three great life goals since they were children. During the early years we had a more "hands on" approach to teaching these Christian values. For years Janet and I had a weekly time of teaching with our children. As our children grew older, however, we did less "direct teaching" (family times, devotions, memory work) and more "informal teaching." This fits with our change from role of protector and authority to our role of friend and guide. Teenagers are starting the transition from being taught Christian values in the home to being equipped as an adult by the larger family of God, the church.

Our Teaching Lifestyle

All Christian values can be taught. In Scripture, God has given us three methods by which we can help our teenager grow toward these goals. These methods constitute our teaching lifestyle.

> Hear, O Israel! The Lord is our God, The Lord is one! And you shall love the Lord your God with all your heart and with all your soul and with all your might. And these words, which I am commanding you today, shall be on your heart; and you shall teach them diligently to your sons and shall talk of them when you sit in your house and when you walk by the way and when you lie down and when you rise up. And you shall bind them as a sign on your hand and they shall be as frontals on your forehead. And you shall write them on the doorposts of your house and on your gates.
>
> Deuteronomy 6:4-9

Parents were to love the Lord first and to have God's Word written on their hearts. The next step was to teach these things to their children. Here we find the first principle of teaching Christian values and helping our teenagers grow toward the three great life goals.

Teaching by Example (Modeling)

We are to model these three great life goals for our teenagers. They should be able to see us growing toward these

106

goals in our own lives first. Then we are in a position to help them work toward these goals. Our lives must always fall in line with what we teach our teenagers. No amount of teaching will ever overcome our actions if they don't match our words. Modeling a vital Christian faith is our greatest way to help our teenagers grow toward their three great life goals.

We can model a vital relationship with God by our close walk with God. By this I mean an observable holiness, which includes a deep dependence on God, a vital prayer life, and a commitment to growing in God's Word. Our teenagers can watch us live out the second goal—a vital relationship with others as we reach out in love to brothers and sisters within the family of God and those without.

The teaching we do by our lives—how we treat our spouse, how we accept and forgive others—how we accept and forgive ourselves, will have tremendous impact on our teenagers' lives.

Formal Teaching

A second method of teaching is given in Deuteronomy 6:6, 7. Parents were to teach their children "diligently." This suggests a structured teaching situation; a time set aside by parents to share some specific principles of God's Word with their children. This method of teaching becomes less dominant as our children become teenagers. I am not advocating we stop family devotions. I am saying that as the teenagers debond, they will probably be less interested in this kind of teaching. We continued to have family times that involved teaching once a week until our two oldest girls left home for college. These times became very informal and more sharing of spiritual thoughts than the outright teaching Janet and I did in the earlier days took place. For ideas on informal family times (spiritual sharing with teenagers), I have written a book called *Christian Family Activities for Families with Teenagers*, published by Standard Publishing.

Talking or Informal Teaching

A third method is found in verse seven. God's people were to "talk" about God's work to their children. They were to talk to their children while they were sitting, lying down, walking, and getting up. In other words, they were to teach informally in all of life. Helping our teenagers grow toward three great life goals takes more than our example. It takes more than structured time. It also takes the discussion and application of God's Word of our lives during informal moments.

I find that the informal moments are some of the best teaching situations with our teenage daughters. What better time is there to teach about love than when your teenager is hurting over a broken romance? These informal times are great learning situations because they are *need*-centered. Informal moments tend to be less "preaching" and more heart-to-heart. All teaching must be heart-to-heart. In essence, we share what is in our hearts toward God.

All three methods as fitting together in a teaching lifestyle as shown below.

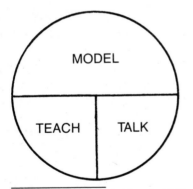

Deuteronomy 6:4-9

Figure 9-1. Model, Teach, Talk

Discussion Questions

1. Finish the sentence, "When I think about influencing the spiritual life of my teenager, I

   _____

   _____ ."

2. What do you see as the greatest obstacle in influencing your teenager's spiritual life?

3. The author gives what he considers to be three great life goals from the teaching of Jesus. Do you agree or disagree that these should be main goals for your teenager's life?

4. In what way are you already helping your teenager work toward these goals?

5. How does Goal 1, a vital relationship with God, affect the other two goals?

6. How does Goal 3, a vital relationship with oneself, affect Goal 2, a vital relationship with others?

7. Of the three methods of teaching given in Deuteronomy 6:4-9, which do you need to increase your skill in most?

8. When you think of "modeling" your Christian faith, how do you feel?

9. What indications are there that your teenager is accomplishing some of the goals to some extent?

10. What one thing will you do to help your teenagers grow towards the three great life goals?

Section Three

The Finishing Touches

CHAPTER 10

Parents in Pain

You are a parent who has had increasing concern about the kind of friends with whom your son is associating. He has been increasingly withdrawn. You try to talk to him but he has little to say. "Maybe he is just going through a stage," you think to yourself, but a nagging feeling inside indicates that you really don't believe it. Things get worse. Your son's grades begin to drop significantly. You confront him once again about his general attitude, and he just says, "I'm OK. Why don't you leave me alone?"

One day the anxiety gets to you. You decide to search his room for any kind of indication of what's going on. You find the evidence—your son is on drugs. Your heart sinks as some of your worst fears come true. Your anxious feelings turn to extreme hurt and anger. "How could he do this to us after all we've done for him? We have given him a warm Christian family. What else could we have done? Where have we gone wrong?"

You are the parent of a teenage daughter. She has been the delight of your eyes. People won over by her sparkling personality. She is a bright, enjoyable daughter with whom you have a good relationship. You have high hopes for her to have a successful Christian life.

The inevitable happens and your daughter starts dating.

You approve of the boy and pleased that your daughter seems to have such good taste. As the romance progresses, you're concerned about the amount of time that your daughter and her boyfriend are spending together. You talk to your daughter about not getting "too serious" because she is just a teenager. The romance continues, with your daughter and her boyfriend getting noticeably closer. You are concerned about the amount of physical contact you're noticing and wonder about what is happening when they are alone. You talk to your daughter about your concerns, but she says, "Oh, Mother—we can handle our relationship. We're not going to get into trouble."

You notice that your daughter is becoming quiet and spending a lot of time in her room. She is not spending as much time around her boyfriend, so you assume that the romance is cooling a bit and she is feeling bad about it. Then the bombshell hits. She tells you that she needs to talk to you and your spouse. You get this sinking feeling in your stomach. Could she be pregnant? Is she on drugs? Has she been sexually abused? You and your spouse sit down with your daughter and she immediately blurts it out: "I'm pregnant."

You sit there in a state of shock. Your emotions surge from desperation to anger, to anxiety, to concern for your daughter, who looks so fragile and broken right now. You immediately think of some of the implications. What will friends and family say? What will happen to the baby? Will she want to marry, and what are the chances of the success of a teenage marriage? Intense anger starts to surface. "How could she have been so self-centered? Why didn't she think about her family? We have spent years, teaching, building close family ties. How could she do this to us?"

There are many other stories of pain. . . .

—You may be the parent of a teenager who has run away several times. Now he tells you he wants to live someplace permanently.

—You may be the parent of a son or daughter that has attempted, or committed, suicide.

—You may be the parent of a teenager who has chosen a completely different lifestyle than yours. His values are those of the world.

114

—You may be a divorced parent, watching your teenager torn between your values and those of your former spouse.

—You may be the parent of a teenager who is running wild. You are bewildered about what to do.

In all of these situations there is one common denominator—*pain.*

Some of you could identify with the illustrations I have given. Some of you have intense pain, others have moderate or little. The illustrations represent people I have known over the years, or my own experiences with my own teenagers. Janet and I know what it is like to feel pain. We have been there—and we ask the inevitable question, "Why me?"

Seven Painful Questions Parents Ask

Why Me?

"Why me?" is a questions that I believe all parents who have suffered significant pain have asked. We say, "Lord, haven't I been faithful to you? Haven't I raised my children in your Word? I have tried so hard to build Christian character into their lives."

"Why me?" is a question that Janet and I asked when we were having pain over one of our daughters. I can remember thinking, "After all the time I have spent with the child, it seems like this should not have happened." Oh, I can remember thinking about the parents I knew that didn't spend half the time or have half the commitment, but their teenagers seemed to be doing fine. It just didn't seem fair.

Part of the answer to this question came one Sunday as I was sitting in the congregation listening to the choir. As I looked down the rows, I started remembering the various kinds of pain that people I knew had experienced or were experiencing. I quickly calculated that about 80% of the people in the choir had experienced or were experiencing significant pain in their lives. I thought, "Wayne, who are you to think that you are exempt from trials in your life?" I was reminded that pain is not a respecter of persons or titles and visits all of us in our lives. Life is not always fair from our perspective.

What Did I Do Wrong?

"What did I do wrong?" is a nagging question that pain over teenagers elicits. This question carries with it the belief that if my teenager has done something wrong I must have done something wrong in raising him. This is an incorrect belief system. We need to be careful in claiming credit for their success or blame for their failures. Generally speaking, good Christian parenting will produce children with few problems. We all know exceptions to this general rule. I have known outstanding children to come out of absolutely terrible families and hardened criminals to emerge from loving Christian homes.

Several factors contribute to this enigma. First and foremost is that God has given our children free will. They are free to choose right and wrong for themselves. In the early years we have greater influence and control on their choices. In the teenage years we have less control and less influence as they become independent. There is a great risk when imperfect people choose for themselves, but that is the way that God has ordered His creation.

In the beginning, God gave His children Adam and Eve the right to choose between good and evil. Even though they had the perfect Father (God) and the perfect family environment (the garden of Eden, reflecting God's love) they chose to sin and bring great pain to their Father. Adam and Eve also had to suffer the consequences. Did Adam and Eve's sin mean that their heavenly Father was at fault for poor parenting? Of course not. Adam and Eve gave in to their selfishness and sinned. Likewise, our children have the freedom to choose godly actions or ungodly actions—a Christ-centered life or a world-centered life. As parents, our responsibility is to provide them with an environment where they will have every opportunity to hear and observe what God wants for their lives. Once we have provided this with love and discipline, we have done all we can do. We can only be responsible *to* our children, not *for* all of their choices.

What Can I Do About My Emotions?

Parents in pain experience what I call the "big five" emotions—hurt, anger, depression, resentment, and guilt. What can you do about these emotions? First, don't try to repress them. Stifling emotions because we believe it's the "right" thing to do can often damage us and our teenagers. These buried emotions tend to go underground and surface in passive-agressive ways, such as, distance, coolness, withholding of affection, etc.

Be honest with yourself, with God, and with selected others on how you're really feeling. Express these emotions in appropriate ways. Express them to yourself. "I am really feeling rage today." Express your emotions to God. "God, I am angry today. I feel so hurt. God, bring some healing and understanding to what I am feeling." God already knows how we are feeling, but expressing to an understanding God will do us immeasurable good. We are talking to someone who really understands and cares how we feel.

Express your emotions to others. Find a good friend, or in some cases a Christian counselor. Find someone who will listen and not necessarily give advice or admonish. Parents in pain need their feelings loved, not instructed.

Some of you are thinking, "What about expressing our emotions to our teenagers?" I am not omitting this, but after the initial confrontations and expressions of emotions, it is often counterproductive to keep expressing them. There is a point where all has been expressed that needs to be expressed. Subsequent emotions on our part have to be taken care of in other ways.

The end result of expression should be resolution. Our purpose in all this work with our emotions is to move on to healing and forgiveness. While we are in the expression stage, we should make a commitment to this goal. I can remember discussing with Janet the difference in the way we were handling our emotions. Hers were not as volatile, nor did they need as much expression, as mine. I recall saying, "I realize I am expressing a lot of anger, but my intent is to forgive. I am not going to stay at this stage." It took longer for me than for Janet to move to resolution, but I believe it was necessary to stay on my own schedule.

Who Really Cares and Understands?

When Janet and I were going through our times of pain, we had several couples in the church to whom we could talk. These people really cared and understood. They did not offer false promises or undesired counsel. They were just there to listen and say, "We care."

We know that God cares and ministers to our needs. One of the ways He ministers to us is through others in the body of Christ.

I cannot emphasize enough the need for such support when parents are in pain. Many are ashamed, or believe that the matter should remain private, or believe people would not want to take the time to help. These are all incorrect beliefs. We know that in the body of Christ healing comes from encouraging one another and building one another up. Parents in pain need people who care. Unfortunately, often our churches do not offer support for parents in pain. It will probably be your responsibility to find someone who can talk to and receive support from. Even though you will not feel like reaching out when you are in pain, assert yourself and find a support group. This will assist in your road toward healing. It is a well-documented fact that healthy families are those that reach out for help in a time of crisis.

How Can I Pray?

This is great power in prayer. Jesus said to His disciples, "If you abide in Me, and My words abide in you, ask whatever you wish and it will be done for you" (John 14:7). We can ask for God's power to be focused on our teenager, and we can trust that God will answer that prayer.

We cannot, however, expect God to force His will on our teenager, because that is not within God's nature. God brings people to a place of decision, but the decision is always up to them. Your teenager has probably been blinded by the gods of this age. "The god of this world has blinded the minds of the unbelieving, that they might not see the light of the gospel of the glory of Christ, who is the image of God" (2 Corinthians 4:4). We can pray that God will restore sight to their blind eyes and they will see the benefits of God's ways more clearly. We can pray that they will respond to this restored sight by abiding in Jesus.

When we pray we really need to turn our teenager over to God. This is difficult to do. We need to say, "God, I give my teenager back to You. His life is in Your hands. I place my complete trust in You that You are working in the life of my teenager. Do with my teenager what You must do to bring him back to You."

How Can I Restore the Relationship?

The kind of pain we have been talking about often separates parents from teens. It is difficult not to take the actions of our teens personally. How can we restore a broken relationship? The answer is both simple and difficult— *forgiveness.* Forgiveness is crucial to dealing with pain. God's Word says, "Be kind to one another, tender-hearted, forgiving each other, just as God in Christ also has forgiven you" (Ephesians 5:32). Our forgiveness came as a gift through Jesus Christ. We did not earn it. There is no way we can repay God for our sins.

The same principles apply to restoring a relationship with our teenagers. Restoration will probably not come through them making things right with us. That might happen at some time, but not soon. The foundation for restoring the relationship will come through us looking at them the way God looks at us. God forgave us in spite of our sins. God continues to forgive us in spite of our sins. We must look at our teenagers as imperfect people who have made mistakes that have hurt us deeply, but who need our forgiveness.

Now I am not saying that the relationship will be restored to normal merely through our forgiveness. All relationships are two-sided. There must be some movement towards you from your teenager. You can only bring the relationship back so far. But that is all you're responsible for. You cannot live your life and your teenager's life too. The relationship might not be all you want it to be for now. Only your forgiveness and a repentant spirit on the side of your teenager will bring complete healing to the relationship.

What Good Can Come From All of This?

You have heard the saying, "no pain, no gain," but where

is all the gain from the pain one can experience from being the parents of a teenager? There are three ways in which we can gain from the pain. The first gain is from the maturity God will build in us from being tested. James 1:2-8 says,

> Consider it all joy, my brethren, when you encounter various trials, knowing that the testing of your faith produces endurance. And let endurance have its perfect result, that you may be perfect and complete, lacking in nothing. But if any of you lacks wisdom, let him ask of God, who gives to all men generously and without reproach, and it will be given to him. But let him ask in faith without any doubting, for the one who doubts is like the surf of the sea driven and tossed by the wind. For let not that man expect that he will receive anything from the Lord, being a double-minded man, unstable in all his ways.

Testing that comes as a result of your teenager will produce perseverance. When you persevere (keep on keeping on) God will develop maturity in you. It is God's desire that we be complete or Christlike in our character. This completeness comes through testing. Because of this we can see joy in the midst of pain. We will not always feel *happiness,* because happiness is a feeling based on current circumstances. Joy, on the other hand, is the assurance we feel that God is always in control, working out His will in our lives. Joy comes from a decision to trust God.

If we do not have this perspective, James says we can ask for wisdom. The wisdom spoken of here is a divine wisdom—God's perspective on testing situations. However, if we fight the testing by becoming bitter, then we become doubters and we will not receive spiritual growth from the Lord.

Our pain helps us minister to others. Because you have suffered pain in raising your teenagers, you will be in a position to help other parents. Paul wrote, "Blessed be the God and Father of our Lord Jesus Christ, the Father of mercies and the God of all comfort, who comforts us in all our affliction so that we may be able to comfort those who are in any affliction with the comfort with which we ourselves are comforted by God" (2 Corinthians 1:3, 4).

When God comforts us we are able to take that same

comfort and help others who are hurting. As a hurting parent of a teenager, you will be able to be of significant help to not only other hurting parents, but to people in all kinds of pain.

Your pain is really gain—for you and others. God uses all circumstances for our good and the good of others, even those circumstances that involve the deep pain caused by our teenagers.

Discussion Questions

1. What could your teenagers do that would cause you the most pain? What would your first response be to such an action? What would you think? How would you feel?

2. What are some answers to "Why me?"

3. How can a parent deal with the question, "What did I do wrong?"

4. What two emotions would you feel the strongest as a parent in pain? How would you express those emotions? What would you struggle with?

5. If you are married, how would you handle the difference between the ways you and your spouse resolve hurt?

6. When you have deep pain in your family, do you tend to find someone with whom to share or do you keep it within the family? Why?

7. How would (do) you pray for a teenager who is choosing sinful ways?

8. Finish the sentence, "The greatest difficulty I have with forgiveness when I have been hurt is

_____

_____ ."

9. What do you need to hear most of what the author said about "What good can come from all of this?"

10. "A new insight to me is _____

and because of this insight, I will _____

_____ ."

CHAPTER 11

The Cluttered Nest

For some time now Janet and I have been looking forward to the empty nest. We certainly have enjoyed our children but we also enjoy the increasing amount of time we can spend together as our children have grown older.

We have mentioned the anticipated bliss of having our children grown and out of the nest to some of our older friends who have already arrived at this "promised land." Most of them have laughed and said, "Don't kid yourself. The empty nest is a myth. Every time we think our nest is empty one of the birds flies back. We just get used to the routine of only the two of us and it is interrupted with the great news, 'Hi, Mom and Dad. Guess what? I've decided to live at home for a while.'"

The Empty Nest Has Been Replaced

According to a study published in a recent issue of the *USC Journal of Sociology and Social Research,* 59% of persons ages 18-24 lived with their parents in 1983, compared to only 46% in 1960. The study, titled, "The Cluttered Nest," was co-authored by USC professors David Heer, Robert Hodge, and Marcus Felson.[1]

The nest becomes cluttered in three primary ways—when royalty returns from college, when royalty never leaves, and when there is a surprise visit from royalty.

When Royalty Returns From College

I have given children who clutter the nest the tongue-in-cheek label of "royalty" because of how they often come home expecting that their return will bring great rejoicing in the kingdom and expecting royal treatment. Sometimes I wonder if they all read the story of the prodigal son before returning home.

It was obvious that Heidi, our first to leave the nest for college, saw herself as royalty when she returned home from college. I will always remember her first trip home at Christmas. We were excited to have her home, but Janet and I quickly realized that what Heidi expected from this time at home and what we as parents expected was vastly different. It seemed that Heidi thought she was doing her mother a favor when she would make messes and leave them for Janet to pick up. In some way Heidi must have believed this would help her mother feel needed once again. Not so! Janet felt used and unappreciated, especially when she realized Heidi was using the Rickerson house as an all-service hotel, just to drop in now and then when she needed or a good solid meal to catch a few winks of sleep between seeing friends. Needless to say, there was conflict over the difference in expectations in the cluttered Rickerson nest.

It is difficult to have children partly in and partly out of the family. When our children first leave for college, they are physically gone but psychologically present—that is, we talk about them frequently and think about them often. As time goes on, we are able to allow them to leave both physically and psychologically. But when they return, the in-out issues return with all the accompanying expectations and feelings.

You can take two steps to lessen the stress of having a college child home. The first step you are already taking by becoming aware of the issues surrounding the cluttered nest. The second thing you can do is to sit down with your college-age son or daughter and work out your differing expectations. This approach is much healthier and productive than carrying around resentment about unmet expectations. We found with Heidi that we let things slide by and became more resentful as the time went on. We had expected her to come home and spend time with the family. She had expected to come home and use the house as a base for her activities. Neither expectations were necessarily wrong, but we did need to express our wants and work out a suitable compromise. I suggest sitting down with your college-age child and discussing the "big three" issues that arise when royalty returns from college. These issues are hours, family time, and chores.

Have a discussion with your college age child about the "big three."

Hours. Your college-age child by now is probably not used to any restrictions at all on his coming and going. There has been no curfew. It will be a significant change for him to come home and find that you still expect him to tell you when he is going to be in or for you to insist on a curfew. Should there be any restriction at all on hours? What about communication about hours? Should the parent be advised as to when the college-age student will be in? What is a workable compromise?

Family time. Even though your child will be glad to be home, the amount of actual family time he feels a need for might be limited compared to what you want and expect. A big priority will be spending time with friends he has not seen for some time. How much family time do both of you expect? What is a reasonable amount of time to be spent with the family? Do you need a schedule for meals, family time, etc? What is a workable compromise?

Chores. In addition to these differences will be the issue of chores. Since your son or daughter has not been a part of the division of labor in your home (if there is one), then you cannot expect him to automatically be sensitive to doing his share. In fact, if Janet and my experience in this area is normal, you can expect your college child *not* to be sensitive. With what chores, as a parent, do you expect help, that if neglected will probably cause irritation and possible resentment? What do you, as a college student, think is reasonable for parents to expect? What is a mutually satisfactory arrangement for chores? How will it be handled if chores are not being done?

This time of communication can be productive as you continue to work out the debonding phase and restructure your relationship with your college-age child. Heidi returned from college after her junior year to live with us for the summer and intern with the church. We worked through most of the issues listed here and because of clear expectations, had an excellent summer. This kind of communication pays off.

When Royalty Never Leaves
When a child decides to stay at home for an extended period of time after high-school graduation, there are issues to be resolved. In some ways, this situation is easier than the coming and going of college students because a suitable arrangement can be developed that remains fairly stable. When the college student comes home, it breaks a routine and there is a time of adjustment. When a child comes home, he has changed in some way and the parents must adjust to that change. When a child stays at home, the changes are less threatening because parts can adjust to them more gradually.

While there may not be the ups and downs of the college student returning, there are still similar significant changes to resolve. For example, when a child graduates from high school, there is the exhilarating feeling that "I'm free." In a sense, graduation from high school is the initiation into the adult world. Most students are 18 or close when they graduate and in our society that allows them most of the privileges of adulthood. At this age, graduates are considered adults. They can vote, get married without parental approval, and in some states purchase alcohol. For the first time, it is feasible for many teenagers to move out and be on their own.

These changes do alter the way our children look at living at home. If they choose to stay, they want the privileges of an adult, but sometimes without the responsibilities of an adult—such as cooking their own meals, doing their own laundry, and paying board and room. Most of the time, parents are not prepared for these changes. They happen suddenly and we *react*. A better way of adjusting to royalty never leaving is to work out our expectations from the outset. Acting in advance will minimize some of the issues that you can sit down with your adult child and discuss.

Finances. What is expected in the area of finances? Will board and room be paid? How much is reasonable? Will a family car be used? If so, what will be the financial arrangements?

Adult freedom. What do I expect from my parents in terms of adult freedom? Will there be a curfew? I might note here that even adult freedom usually means being responsible to check schedules and let others know where they are. Is there a difference between the responsibility between a husband and wife and an adult child and his parents? What is a balance you can live with?

Equal participation. Since all are adults, what will be expected of each in terms of tasks? What about meals, laundry, cleaning?

Family time. What are the expectations for family time? What do both parties want in terms of maintaining the relationships? What is the balance?

How long? What are the expectations of both on how long the adult child is to be at home? What are the short and long range plans?

A Surprise Visit From Royalty

As I mentioned earlier, many of our friends have had surprise visits from the "royalty" in their families. The dream of increased freedom, solitude, financial freedom and the release from any parenting save the glories of grandparenting is shattered by three words—"I'm coming home." By now the new routine of the empty nest has been firmly established and the announcement, "I'm coming home," is met with mixed reviews. We remain committed to our children and concerned about their welfare, but we have become accustomed to showing our concern from not quite so close a range.

Reasons for adult children returning vary. Some want to live at home for a while to save money while other children need to live at home because of situations resulting from divorce, unemployment, or illness. Whatever the situation, expectations will need to be worked out. One of the changes when adult children return is that they are often very different than when they lived in our homes. These differences can include changes in their lifestyles, values, and independence. Most often our children are adults who want virtually no parenting—with the exception, often, of their mother's cooking, cleaning, and doing laundry.

In the case of returning royalty it is *essential* that there be clear communication of expectations and specific decisions in terms of what the compromise will be in any areas of conflicting expectations.

Questions that need to be covered are:

—What will be the financial arrangements?

—What will be the division of labor?

—How long will this arrangement be for?

—What will need to be communicated in terms of hours and schedules?

—Are there differences in values or lifestyles that will need to be worked out?

—What is *essential* for this new arrangement to work? (Have each person say what is most important to him or her.)

In a word, the single most important element in making the cluttered nest work is *communication*. Assuming that one another will automatically know what is expected will only bring hurt and resentment. The hard work of communication, however, will provide the foundation for healthy relationships.

---

[1]*Marriage and Divorce Today,* Vol. 10, No. 50, July 15, 1985, p. 1.

Discussion Questions

1. Finish the statement, "When I think about the 'Empty Nest' I feel

   _____ ."

2. What is your greatest concern about the "Empty Nest"?

3. How do you feel about having a "Cluttered Nest"?

4. What is your greatest concern about having a "Cluttered Nest"?

5. How do you believe "royalty" returning from college will affect your family?

6. What is the greatest issue you would face if "royalty" never leaves?

7. Visualize your home if you had a surprise visit from "royalty." What would happen?

8. What is a "non-negotiable" with you when your next becomes cluttered?

9. If you are married, what possible tension could you see between you and your spouse over the "Cluttered Nest" issued?

10. As a result of this information, I will take the following step to prepare for the "Cluttered Nest":

CHAPTER 12

Finally Friends

This morning the phone rang before 7:00 a.m. as I was getting ready to leave for work. My wife answered the phone and I quickly realized that it was Liesl, our daughter calling from Los Angeles. It is not unusual to have Liesl call a couple of times a week and talk to her mother (and sometimes to her dad) because, you see, they are finally friends—in fact, best of friends.

Janet and Liesl have not always been the best of friends. Liesl was a strong-willed and often rebellious teenager. There were a lot of power struggles in our home and when it came to Liesl and Janet, Liesl often prevailed. Now that debonding is no longer an issue, the need to pull away from the family is no longer there for Liesl. She has secure family of her own with a husband and one-year-old daughter, Stephanie.

When our children finally finish the task of debonding and have a more secure sense of identity, the stage is set for being finally friends. I am not saying that we have not been friends with our children until this stage. Hopefully we have been building a special kind of friendship that will continue to grow over the years. What I am saying is that the nature of our friendship changes when our children have debonded. The finally friends kind of friendship that I am talking about is a more mature friendship, free from the hierarchical parent-child dynamic. This new kind of freedom is more like the one that we have with those close friends outside the family. It is a friendship that we develop because we *choose* a close relationship with that person. This kind of friendship is free from the psychological guilt of a relationship with parents that is a result of "shoulds" ("I should call," "I should visit").

During early adolescence, 75% of our relationship with our children is more hierarchical in nature and 25% is more of a friendship nature. As our children grow through independence our parent/friendship ratio changes until, in the "finally friends" stage, we are more like 75% friend and 25% parent (these are arbitrary percentages that I use only to show changes).

It might be helpful here to visualize this change in the parent/friendship transition through the use of the Dependence/Independence chart I used in Chapter 4.

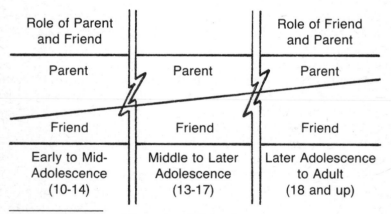

Role of Parent and Friend		Role of Friend and Parent
Parent	Parent	Parent
Friend	Friend	Friend
Early to Mid-Adolescence (10-14)	Middle to Later Adolescence (13-17)	Later Adolescence to Adult (18 and up)

Figure 12-1. Role of Parent and Friend

It is not all easy giving up our role as parent first, friend second. Even when we consciously work at changing the 75/25 factor to 25/75, some parenting urges overwhelm us. On the other hand are those "I want to be parented" urges on the part of grown children. I don't think we ever completely get over the desire for approval from our parents. I can remember taking my latest book to my parents and feeling somewhat like a child during "show and tell." And I was in my forties! If this need for approval is too great then it can interfere with our mental health.

Alan McGinniss, in his book, *The Friendship Factor*, speaks of this difficult, but necessary, shift that must occur in the parent/friend ratio with our children. "A great Scandinavian actress with worldwide fame and with a daughter of her own, was asked if she could relate to her mother as one adult to another. 'I would love to,' she said. 'It's my big dream. But my mother insists to be the mother and I am the daughter. She does it without knowing it, because she claims she doesn't do it, and that's the way it will be forever, you know. Maybe it's my fault, too, because also without knowing it, I think I cater to being the daughter. But I really would love to have her as a friend. I would love to know who she really is. What are her thoughts, her disappointments, her hopes, as a woman—not as a mother I know, but as a woman.'"[1]

I believe it takes a conscious effort to develop the kind of relationship that the Scandinavian actress so intensely desired with her mother. The shift in relationship from parent/friend to friend/parent is a deliberate process. Part of that process includes *unlearning* previous parenting tendencies that were necessary when our children were young. To help you make that transition, following are seven characteristics of an intimate friendship.

Qualities of Friendship

A Friend Is Not Possessive

"Love ... is not jealous" (1 Corinthians 13:4). Friendship should include the free giving of self to one another. True love does not want to "own" the other person. Love does not demand certain expectations of another person and then act devastated when the friend does not deliver. A possessive love with our children would be one in which we expect them to call or write according to our schedule and then pile guilt upon them when they don't live up to our expectations. A non-possessive love releases our children to create a world of their own and then counts it a blessing when we are included in that world.

A Friend Is Loyal

Loyalty means sticking by another person no matter what the circumstances. Loyalty is love based on commitment to the other person even when the friend disappoints you. Loyalty is acceptance without the conditions of a certain level of performance. The kind of friendship we need to develop with our children is one where they no longer feel the need to work for our approval. Proverbs 17:17 says it well—"A friend loves at all times, and a brother is born for adversity."

A Friend Listens, Not Lectures

This characteristic of friendship does not come easy to parents. This is an area where we must *unlearn* an old habit—lecturing, in order to become a friend who listens. I find myself figuratively having to sit on my hands to not give advice to my children. When I see them moving in unwise directions, I want to revert to the old lecture style. It is certainly legitimate to give counsel at times, but often we are too free with our wisdom. Our children need to be given the freedom to make mistakes and learn from those mistakes like we did.

One of the characteristics I appreciate most in a good friend of mine, Jeff Bisaga, is that he just listens to my rantings and ravings. He doesn't lecture or offer advice, even though I know he is often tempted to. He gives counsel only when he sees I am open to it or feels strongly that I need to be confronted. To be "finally friends" with our children, we need to develop that listening that is "quick to hear, slow to speak" (James 1:19).

A Friend Confronts But Is Not Critical

This characteristic of friendship is what the apostle Paul calls "speaking the truth in love" (Ephesians 4:15). A real friend confronts when it is the loving thing to do, not out of personal hurt or vindictiveness. A friend chooses carefully the area to be confronted and yet cares enough to confront when needed and risk the anger of the friend.

As parents we need to *unlearn* inappropriate confrontation over less significant or personally irritating things and save our confrontation for times when we feel strongly convicted that God wants us to confront. When we confront too often over minor issues, our children revert to their earlier listening habits—deaf ears. If our confrontations are few and far between, our children will realize that when we do confront, it is something we believe they really need to hear.

A Friend Is Affirming

Most of us provide our children with more reminding, rebuking, telling, and suggesting than affirmation. As we encourage our children towards excellence in all areas of their lives we often forget to affirm them for *who they are*, regardless of what they are achieving at the moment. In a 75%-friend, 25%-parent kind of relationship we need to develop the trait of affirmation. The Scripture says to use words "for building others up in accordance to their needs" (Ephesians 4:29). Determine to develop a regular habit of affirming your adult child.

A Friend Is Open

A hierarchical type of relationship, such as most of us had with our children when they were growing up, is not very conducive to openness. A mature, intimate friendship is based upon equals in a relationship taking risks by sharing what is deep inside.

Your children want to know the real you. Now is the time to start developing that kind of openness that few friendships have. You can start sharing with your adult children your struggles, your fears, your spiritual battles, your feelings of inadequacy, your deepest wishes and values. When our children were growing up, we often protected them from such openness. They were not ready for such levels of sharing. Now they are ready! And with such openness comes a wonderful "finally friends" relationship.

A Friend Shares Activities

Friendships are based to some degree on shared activities that bring enjoyment to both parties. With Janet and our daughters that activity is definitely shopping. They all claim that same "spiritual gift." I mean those girls no more than hit the door and shopping plans are being made. You can just feel the excitement. I believe all of us can find at least one mutually enjoyable activity that we can share with our adult children. These shared activities will deepen that "finally friends" bond.

Conclusion

I think it is fitting that this book end with a look at friendship and discussions in Chapter 13 that will enhance an intimate relationship. From the time our children were born, it has been our task to raise those children as a parent and friend. It is this combination that, though it varied at times, enables us to have the greatest joy on earth—*family.*

---

[1]Alan L. McGinniss, *The Friendship Factor.* Minneapolis, MN: Augsburg, 1979, p. 80.

Discussion Questions

1. When you think of the phrase "a friend to my child," what are your feelings?

2. The author talks about the 75/25 factor (75% parent, 25% friend) in our relationship. What is the percentage factor with your teenager right now?

3. How do you think your teenager would rate the percentage factor of your friendship?

4. What is the percentage factor with *your* parents right now. Are you satisfied or would you change the percentage?

5. Finish the statement, "One thing I would change about my friendship with my parents is

   _____

   _____ ."

6. On a scale of 1—10, how well do you live out the characteristic, "a friend is not possessive" with your teenager?

7. On a scale of 1—10, how well do you live out the characteristic, "a friend listens, not lectures."

8. Which of the seven characteristics of friendship given by the author is most difficult for you to live out with your teenager?

9. What growth have you seen in your friendship with your teenager in the last year?

10. What one thing will you do to improve your friendship with your teenager?

CHAPTER 13

Structured Discussions Between Parents and Teens

This final chapter will provide you with an opportunity to review the concepts in each of the twelve preceding chapters and choose the areas you believe are most important for you to work on. This chapter will also give you strategy for discussing important issues directly with your teenager. Make sure your teenager realizes this is not a lecture but actually a give-and-take session where he and you alike can share thoughts, feelings, and wants. If your teenager sees these sessions as a way for you to make him "shape up" in a given area then your time together will probably be unproductive. The main goal of these sessions should be increased *understanding*—your understanding of your teen and your teen's of you.

CHAPTER 1—How Can We Be Prepared?

1. On a scale of 1—10, with ten being "very tolerant," have your teenager choose a number that indicates how tolerant he believes you are. Ask him to tell you in what areas he believes you are most intolerant and how you could become more tolerant.

2. Review the emotions that the author says most parents of teenagers experience and share your strongest emotion with your teenager. Discuss your feelings in depth.

CHAPTER 2—"It's Different Now!"

Fill out the difference chart on page 28 and discuss it with your teenager. Talk about what it was like when you were a teenager in each of the ten areas. Ask your teenager if he agrees with your assessment of how the world is different today, or if he sees differences you have not seen.

CHAPTER 3—"Mirror, Mirror on the Wall, Who Am I?"

Ask your teenager to rate his self-esteem on a scale of 1—10 as follows:

Feel terrible   Feel great
about myself   about myself

1   2   3   4   5   6   7   8   9   10

Discuss: When do you feel best about yourself? When do you feel worst about yourself? As a parent share some of your feelings of self worth when you were a teenager.

CHAPTER 4—"I Don't Need You Anymore"

On page 50 is a Dependence/Independence Scale. Make a copy for yourself and for your teenager. Fill these out and compare your results. How do you rate one another in terms of releasing or being released? "Too slow," "Too fast," or "Just about right." Discuss your differences. If your teenager rates the way you are releasing him/her as too slow or too fast, ask what you could do differently that would help.

CHAPTER 5—How to Listen So Your Teenager Will Talk

The author gives three obstacles to listening: judging, preparing, and lecturing. Share these three obstacles with your teenager and ask, "Which do you think is an obstacle in my listening?" Have your teenager complete the following open-end statement—"It would be easier for me to talk to you if you would _____

_____."

Complete the following open-ended statement for your teenager—"It would be easier for me to listen to you if you would _____

_____ .

Each of you make a commitment to change one area that will improve listening between you.

CHAPTER 6—How to Talk So Your Teenager Will Listen

You and your teenager should each prepare one "Straight Talk" statement.

"I feel _____ when _____

because _____ ."

Discuss these statements. Discuss the benefits of using "Straight Talk" statements to better understand one another.

CHAPTER 7—Too Big to Spank

Ask your teenager, "How will you discipline your teenagers when you have children?" "What changes will you make from how you have been disciplined by us?" Share with your teenager your biggest frustration with disciplining a teenager.

CHAPTER 8—Hormones, Dating, and Love

Work out a dating policy with your teenager. Thirteen questions are given in Chapter 8 for you and your teenager to answer. Answer them separately, then work out the policy in a session or series of sessions. Have your teenager make a copy of the policy for himself and for you.

CHAPTER 9—Three Great Life Goals for Teenagers

Share with your teenager three great life goals for teenagers (really, for everyone). Read Matthew 22:37-40 together. You and your teenager rate yourselves on at what point you are in achieving those goals. Rate yourself on a scale of 1—10 with ten being "Goal Achieved."

Goal 1—A vital relationship with God
Goal 2—A vital relationship with others
Goal 3—A vital relationship with self

Ask your teenager what you could do to encourage him in any of those areas.

CHAPTER 10—Parents in Pain

Teenagers often do not have a very clear sense of the pain we sometimes feel over their behavior. Complete the following open-ended sentences and share them with your teenager.

"My greatest fear for your life is _____

_____ ."

"I feel the most pain when _____

_____ ."

CHAPTER 11—The Cluttered Nest

Included in Chapter 11 are discussion questions for families with children in college, children who have graduated from high school, and children who have returned home to live. Discuss any of those areas that are relevant to your situation now or to prepare for the future.

CHAPTER 12—Finally Friends

Discuss with your teenager how you can become better friends. Ask each other the question, "What could I do to become better friends with you?" Discuss together in what ways does our relationship need to change to move from parent/child to friend/friend? What is our greatest obstacle to friendship?

In this book we have discussed many parenting issues. It is easy to become overwhelmed by the many areas we see that could be improved. Let me remind you of what I said earlier in the book, that we need to go on ourselves and take just one small step at a time. If you could choose just *one area* to work on for the next year, that would be a significant step of growth in your parenting. We grow by the PINCH—that is, a *Parent Inch.* By this I mean that our growth is a little at a time; slow and often painful. Take just one PINCH during the next twelve months and God will bless your efforts.

Discussion Questions

This is a review chapter with structured discussion for you and your teenager. If you are going through this book on your own, choose one structured discussion area you will share with your teenager.

If you are in a small parenting group, be ready to discuss the following:

1. What do I think will be the most difficult area for me to discuss with my teenager?

2. Which area do I want to avoid? Why?

3. What area is first on my priority list to discuss with my teenager?

4. What must I personally do to make these discussions successful?

5. "I commit myself to discuss ____*(discussion area)*____

_____ with my teenager."